BECOMING A FRIEND OF GOD

BECOMING A FRIEND OF GOD

STORIES OF REAL PEOPLE WHO FOUND GOD

LARRY KEEFAUVER   DAVID YOUNGREN

DAVID GARCIA   ALLAN EARLS

DANA WILLIAMS   RICCO MCADORY

JEFF GOLDEN   LINDA OPPERMAN

BOB ENGLEHART   MIKE MAC MCKOY

SUSAN J. BILY-LINDNER

FRIEND OF GOD BOOKS

CONTENTS

INTRODUCTION - BECOMING GOD'S FRIEND

GOD FOUND ME...

Years ago, a major church denomination had an evangelistic campaign called, "I found it." I {Dr. Larry Keefauver} found it somewhat offensive. The "it" I think they were referring to was "salvation" or "Good News" or whatever. However, their assumption seemed to be that the person who put that bumper sticker on their vehicle had discovered *something* significant. The person seeing the sticker would then be curious to ask what the statement meant and then the Christian could share "it" with the seeker.

I have great news for you. The people sharing their stories in this book have not found *something*...rather, they have been sought out and found by *Someone*!

God found me; first, in my bedroom when I was eleven years old. While I had been going to Sunday School and Church since cradle roll, I had found all that stuff boring as a kid. And, I had tried reading a King James Bible but understood very little in it about God. When I told my parents about my boredom and that I didn't want to go to church, they did two things—made me go to church (ugh!) and required me to read *Egermeier's Bible Story Book*. I loved the pictures and became fascinated with the stories. In fact, I would read it through over and over again for the next few years until I knew most of the stories by heart.

A particular story intrigued me. An Old Testament prophet, Isaiah, was in the Temple and mourning the death of his friend, the King of Israel. Suddenly the presence of God filled the Temple, angels appeared worshipping God, and the divine voice spoke to Isaiah, "Whom shall I send?" Isaiah was troubled by his people, the Israelites, and how they had abandoned their worship of the Living God. They needed to hear the truth about God and His ways. God needed someone to tell them about His Truth and Love. When God asked, "Whom shall I send?" ... Isaiah responded, "Here am I, send me."

After reading that story for the nth time, I was strangely touched one night before falling asleep. Filled with awe, I wondered, "Was such an experience of God possible for me?"

In the middle of the night, I was awakened by loud, thundering noises and a room filled with fiery light. I experienced God's presence and sensed Him saying to me exactly what He had asked Isaiah centuries ago. Deep within my heart, I responded, "God, here am I, send me." I knew deep within me that I would somehow serve Him with my life and go around the globe sharing about my friend, the Living God of Abraham, Isaac, and Jacob...and His Son, Jesus the Christ.

Now over sixty years later, I can share with you that God is a BFF...Best Friend Forever. He has given me a wonderful wife, children, grandchildren, Christian friends, great colleagues in publishing, writing, and churches throughout the world. My Best Friend Forever has inspired me along with my wife, Judi, to write over sixty book and curricula which are out there around the world in eleven languages with over two million-plus published. All because my friend, God, found me and offered an eternal relationship with Him through Jesus the Christ. Wow! What a friend I have in Jesus the Son, God the Father, and the Holy Spirit.

Becoming a Friend of God

How do you become a friend of God? The *How* is a process unique to each individual. The stories about the friends of God can be read in the scriptures...Moses, Rahab, Abraham and Sarah, David, Esther, David, Hannah, Isaiah, Mary and Elizabeth, the disciples, Priscilla, Paul, and scores of others. God's friends throughout the Early Church and Church history have been martyrs, saints, and the worst of sinners who were rescued by the risen Christ. In fact, Jesus says to us:

> "No longer do I call you servants, for a servant
> does not know what his master is doing; but
> I have called you friends, for all things that I
> heard from My Father I have made known
> to you."

— JOHN 15:15-16

Meeting God Through a Battered Infant

Experience unconditional love as you seek to become God's friend.

Jessica taught me more about God's seeking love than anyone I have ever known. I met Jessica when she was only three months old and weighed a meager six pounds. Her life had epitomized the tragedy of innocent suffering and pain.

Jessica was born normal with one exception; she had no sucking reflex. Her single, unwed mother had four other children under the age of six when Jessica born. In the hospital, the nurses and aides carefully taught Jessica's mother how to manipulate her jaws and lips to teach her how to such. This took much time, patience and effort. Everything worked well as long as Jessica and her mom were in the hospital. But upon returning back home, Jessica's mom was overwhelmed with all the tasks required now by the care of five children under the age of six including Jessica who couldn't suck properly and thus was forever hungry and crying.

This proved too much for Jessica's mom. She simply didn't have the time to teach baby Jessica how to such. And she had no tolerance for her constant crying and whining. As a result, whenever Jessica cried, she received a hard slap on the face to shut her up. This continued to the point when Jessica could no longer see or hear due to cerebral concussions. Jessica had also learned how to cry on the inside—trembling violently whenever she was hungry or touched.

By the time a social worker discovered Jessica's plight, she was almost dead. Saved by modern medical intervention, Jessica recovered in the hospital NICU unit until she could be fed with a tube by foster parents. Judi and I became those parents. As an RN with neonatal and extensive nursery experience, Judi became the foster caregiver and I became the aide. Spelling my wife on the late-night shifts, I would feed Jessica during the night watches.

At first, when I went in for her scheduled tube feeding, my initial touch of Jessica would prompt her to tremble violently with fear and cry on the inside never making an audible sound. Instead of cuddling, she remained rigid and frightened as I held her. She had never known the presence of another with accompanying pain.

For months I stayed with the drill, maintained the routine, going to Jessica night after night without any sign of a response other than fear and dread. I sang to her as I fed and rocked her. I knew she could feel the vibration of my songs in the night. I would softly speak to her of my love for her. Still, no response.

Then late one night, months after she had first laid in my arms, I picked her up and she didn't tremble with fear or cry in silence. In fact, she cuddled. She cooed. She received the touch and the hug that I offered her. She accepted my comforting and unconditional loving presence into her life.

Some of us are much like Jessica. God's unconditional, loving, seeking presence reaches out to hold us, touch us and comfort us. If we can but stop trembling in fear, crying in silence and resisting his touch, we will be made whole in his presence. Though Jessica never saw my face physically, we met face to face in love and touched one another heart to heart. All who touched him were made whole.

Look up into His loving face. Receive his healing touch. God's presence hugs you with unconditional love and seeks to make you whole.

What keep you from opening the door and letting God's loving presence heal you?

Take a journey with each writer in this book. Experience the reality of becoming a friend of God through their lives. And then... become a friend of God sharing His love with everyone in your life.

DR. LARRY KEEFAUVER

A FAMILY MEMBER BECOMES
A FRIEND OF GOD

BY DR. LARRY KEEFAUVER

I t's supernatural...it's a miracle when a family member become a friend of God.

In 1999, I have a nightmare of seeing my brother at the Great White Throne judgment in the midst of the lost. His look at me across the abyss caused me to wake up suddenly in a cold sweat and trembling.

I went to my office and prayed, "Lord, why isn't my brother saved?" The Spirit responded, "What is it in you that keeps Al from being saved?"

Then, I started writing down all the walls in me that kept my brother from Jesus and resulted in a book, *Lord I Wish My Family Would Get Saved*, published in 2000 by Creation House and still in print.

Subsequently, the book was published in Mandarin, Indonesian, and Portuguese. I traveled all over Asia, the US, Canada, and Brazil preaching and teaching on family salvation. At 100 Huntley Street with David Mainse, I spent 1 week on their programs speaking about the book. They asked their viewers and partners to send in pictures and prayer request for family member salvations. Over 400,000 requests were received which papered the walls of their chapel, studio and common area during which staff prayed daily for salvations.

Additionally, over $100,000 CAD came into the network building memorial offerings based on Acts 10 for family salvation. Tens of thousands of testimonies came in during the year of salvations. Miracle upon miracle happened. Many churches like Lovejoy in Buffalo set up wailing walls with pictures and prayer letters for family members. Service after service, week after week, congregations would pray for family members to be saved and then people would stand up and give testimonies about family members being saved. Some would bring their family members to church and the whole church would rejoice at their baptisms.

I traveled throughout the nations preaching and teaching, and on TV as well through TBN, CTN, Cornerstone, and Daystar I talked about the book and asked viewers and congregants alike to pray for my brother's salvation. Literally, millions were reached with this message and I believe hundreds of thousands did pray.

Then in 2003, Pastor Henry Hinn invited me to come to his church in Vancouver and preach on family salvation. When I mentioned my brother in the message and asked people to pray for him, Henry stood up and gave a prophetic word, "Within a year, your brother will be saved as a result of heart problems."

In November of that year, a church in Spokane, WA, emailed me and Judi asking us to come on Valentine's Day weekend in 2004 to come to a campground outside of Spokane in the mountains to lead a marriage seminar for about 20 couples. We already had personal plans on that weekend for us to celebrate in Florida. We had no desire to travel across the country to do a marriage seminar in the snowy mountains for a few couples.

So, I prepared to write an email declining the request and recommend a couple in the NW who could do the retreat. Judi agreed with me. As I wrote the email the Holy Spirit said to me, "Do the retreat. You will have a divine appointment."

Before I pushed send on the declining email, I told Judi what the Spirit said. She paused and then said, "Okay, we should do it but you had better have heard the Holy Spirit on this!" I accepted the invitation and on so on Friday, Feb. 14, 2003, we boarded an early flight from Orlando to Denver, changed planes and flew on to Spokane, WA. The church's pastor picked us up at the airport and we drove about 2 hrs into the mountains and arrived at a snow-covered campground....cold, cold, cold.

It was a good retreat. Marriages healed. Divorces canceled. All miracles in and of themselves. So, Sunday afternoon, we boarded our cross country red-eye flight back from Spokane to Denver for an hour layover and then fly on to Orlando. Judi asked on the flight, "So what was the divine appointment?" I responded with all the spiritual spin I could muster about healed marriages and canceled divorces but she seemed unconvinced about the critical necessity for us making such a long trip, out of FL during the winter.

When we landed in Denver, I turned on my cell phone and checked for messages. Only one voice mail was on my cell. I listened. It was my brother. I hadn't talked to him on the phone for years. We had exchanged polite emails and Christmas over the years. All of my efforts to reach out to him especially with Christ were rejected. He had thrown my books away and answered my emails with, "The force be with you."

Hearing his voice in the voicemail shocked me. He was weeping and I had no idea how he had gotten my cell number. I learned later he had called my sister, who with the rest of my family, had been praying for him to be saved for years. As a teenager, Al had been hurt by words from a church leader and had walked out of the church and a relationship with the Lord never to return.

I could barely understand Al's message to me broken up by sobs. "Larry, bro, I must talk to you. My heart's broken. Where in the world are you?"

I was stunned. I was listening to this voicemail on my cell standing in the Denver Airport. My brother lived in Denver, just 15 minutes from the airport!

I called him. We talked and I told him I was actually in the Denver airport. He asked me to stay over and talk with him the next morning. I agreed. Judi was thrilled. She flew on to Orlando and I made arrangements to delay my flight and return the next evening. Got a hotel next to the airport and looked forward to reuniting with my brother the next day.

What prompted his phone call to me at just the day I would be in Denver, unknown to him? Millions of prayers and a curious meeting of a woman through an online dating site.

Months before our divine appointment, Al had met Kim online. He was divorced. She was a widow. She lived in Colorado Springs to be close to her brother's family. The week before Valentine's Day, Al had told Kim he loved her and wanted to marry her after dating for months. She said no. She couldn't marry someone whose god wasn't her God. She was a committed, born again Christian.

You need to know that Kim's brother is the President of Focus on the Family which is why they lived in Colorado Springs. The Holy Spirit has really led a secret weapon into Al's life through a dating site of all things!

Anyway, Al's spurned proposal had broken his heart. Just like the prophetic word from Pastor Hinn had prophesied. Heart problems. He had been weeping and unable to go to work or even drive since that rejection.

When Al showed up at the hotel room on Monday morning, I was surprised to see an attractive blond at his side. It was Kim. He had asked her to drive him over to the hotel. The three of us sat on the floor. Weeping he told me his story and how Kim's persistent witness to him over the months hadn't gotten through to him until she said no to him. His hardened heart had been broken and now he was ready to hear from me and her about Christ. We talked. Confessions and tears flowed. Love and forgiveness from the Father and between brothers overflowed. My brother accepted Jesus as Lord and Savior on that hotel bedroom floor and all of us wept, rejoiced, prayed and then went to breakfast at Denny's.

I have never seen in my forty-two years of ministry such a radical, wonderful, instant change in a person. Al was reborn right before our eyes. By the way, the following Easter, I had the privilege to baptize Al in the Atlantic Ocean and officiate the wedding for Al and Kim on the beach in New Smyrna Beach. Now that's a miracle!! That's Supernatural!!

I invite you to begin praying for lost family members. Repent of any walls of anger, rejection, hurt, or pride that may be keeping you separated from a family member who isn't God's friend. God loves them just as He loves you. Let God love your unsaved family members through you. What an awesome miracle it is when a family member who was lost is now found and is become *a friend of God.*

ABOUT DR. LARRY KEEFAUVER

Dr. Larry Keefauver pastored in churches for forty years. He is a bestselling author, editor, coach, speaker and teacher.

drlarrykeefauver@gmail.com
www.doctorlarry.org

DANA WILLIAMS

WITH GOD'S FRIENDS, ALL THINGS ARE POSSIBLE

BY MRS. DANA R. WILLIAMS

God is certainly amazing! God's will for us is already predestined for a purpose and for a great destiny. I received a major blessing within the few months of my birth. I was adopted into the greatest family anyone can ever desire growing up in. Some kids are never adopted or even have the experience to enjoy a loving family. God blessed me with a great mother and father! If they hadn't told I was adopted, I would not have believed it.

I grew up in the admonition of the Lord.

As a little girl, I loved to twirl and whirl and dance to any type of music that would come across the radio or stereo. I would make faces and my parents would take pictures of me.

My father was a sergeant in the US Army. He would come home after work and blow the horn outside in our complex and he would take me for a ride around the block in the big military trucks.

My mom and I enjoyed spending time together baking cookies, playing with little toy boats, and enjoying the local PX and shopping.

As we were walking to the PX to shop, I would speak to anyone we met and give them a big goofy smile.

Usually, their response would be, "She is so cute look at her."

Our life was exciting. We lived all over the United States and we went to Germany two times to live for a total of six years living in Europe. While we were there, my family enjoyed cruising the Rhine River and we enjoyed the October Fest as well as other local festivals and circuses. We also went to Holland and enjoyed their festivals. Our classes were held on base, but we took field trips to see the Berlin Wall. Going on my first ski trip and going on the ski lift was exciting. Most of the time my mother and father would accompany me on these school trips.

When we came back from Germany, I went to a local elementary school. My teacher chose me to hang up the US flag every morning and to take it down every day before school was out. That was truly a special privilege for me.

My mother and father were very inspirational in life. Many of the soldiers my father worked with came over to the house for wise counsel and to visit. My dad was truly a natural-born leader and full of wisdom. My father retired from the Army after serving over twenty years. I really enjoyed it because I had the opportunity to travel, meet new people, and experience many different cultures.

During High School, I was very popular. I enjoyed playing sports. I was on the JV and Varsity Basketball team, track team, and played softball with the local community. I received many awards from the J.R.O.T.C. department and was actively involved in the color guard and the drum corps. It was great playing in the local festivals and making a lot of noise.

The Hand of God

As a young child, I can remember how the hand of God was over my life. When we were stationed in Ft. Benning, Georgia, there was a tornado that touched down two blocks from our house. It sounded like a freight train was coming through our community.

When we were at another post in Georgia, I had the chickenpox and my mother would not let me go outside to play that day so I could recover quickly. When my dad came home, we all went to the store. When we came back, a drunk driver had plowed through our house. It went through the room where I was playing the majority of the day. We were shocked and in utter disbelief. We had to move out of that house and be put into another house on base it was so damaged. God's protection is so amazing!

Experiencing the World

My family took me to church almost every Sunday. Our family was truly a God-fearing family. My great grandfather was a Baptist preacher in the early 1800s. I was active in my local church at an early age. I was the Sunday School Secretary and I also ushered and sang in the choir.

As I grew up and got older, I became curious about what the world had to offer. During High School towards the end of my junior year, I experimented with alcohol and marijuana. No hard drugs because even what little I did was very scary. Also, I didn't have a lot of money to waste on bad habits, so I decided it wasn't worth it.

However, after I graduated from High School, my social circle began to change. Going out to clubs regularly, I began smoking weed and drinking frequently. At the same time, I was going to the local community college. I was accepted into a couple of HBCU Schools, but my family preferred for me to stay home at least for my first year of college.

Back-Up Dancer

There was a new craze that came out in the early '90s called Rump Shaking. Today, it is called Twerking. My best friend and I entered a local contest and we won and split the prize money. After that, we danced at the local night clubs. It was crazy. At this club called New World, many famous artists would come through there. We would meet them because we knew the DJ and we also hung out with the owner's sons. It was there I met so many people like the legendary TUPAC, Kidd Capri, Biz Markie, and Mobb Deep, just to name a few. During that time, we were very popular. Even the neighboring state of South Carolina and the club D.J's would pay for my friend and me to dance at their clubs. We also danced for two local groups as back up dancers. Oh, how I loved to dance and now I was getting paid for it!

There was a controversial group called The Fresh Kidd Ice of the 2 Live Crew that came to the club looking for girls to go on tour and dance with them. We were chosen. We had the best time traveling and meeting even many more artists. We were paid very well. When they would come up from Miami, they pick us up in North Carolina, and we would keep on rolling.

I was a China Doll and we learned how to dance from the baddest strippers out of Miami. We did not bare it all on stage, but we were very sexy. It required staying in shape and rehearsing a lot. Some of the artists we shared the stage with were Naughty by Nature, The 69 Boys, 95 South, Trends of Culture Home Team, and many others. At the time, I thought those were some of the best times in my life. We stayed at the best hotels, traveled, and met so many interesting and famous people. Life seemed full and fun!

Sin is extremely fun until it produces death. Let me tell you, the spirit of death was after me. I could feel it. I was in so many car accidents even prior to going to Atlanta. One car accident was on a bridge. Another time I got hit by a utility truck owned by the city of Wilmington, NC. Yet another time I was hit while in the car with my friends. One night we had been out drinking with friends and our car spun completely around and almost hit the cemetery gate.

Though I was not in the custom of smoking weed, I was at the club and the weed smelled so good, I asked the guy if I could have some and he said yes. It made me so sick and made my heart beat so fast I felt like I was going to die. Laying down in the back of my car, I keep calling on Jesus to help me. My friend came and got me and said she wanted me to meet TUPAC. I met him personally and talked to him, but I was so high, I really don't remember much about it. I could have died that night, but God continued to keep His hand on me.

God had a plan and purpose for my life. He continually watched over me and drew me back toward Him even though I did not know it at the time.

Encounter with the Devil

After a horrible fight with my father, I moved to Atlanta, Georgia with my best friend. Once we got to Atlanta, though, things really get out of control. Without the oversight of my parents, we were just two young women out there on our own. We were working and partying on the weekends as usual. Then I met a guy at my job that I found out later was just completely deceptive and sold out to the devil. My first instincts were right about him, but I had always tried to get along with everyone I worked with.

About this time, I was facing a major decision in my life and I confided in him. Of course, this guy said everything I wanted to hear and agreed with me on how I wanted to handle the situation. He kept encouraging me to open up to him and he let me know he was there for me if I needed him.

After working together for a while, he said he needed my help. He asked if I would let him move his books into my place until he found his own apartment. Most of the books were covered so I really did not pay any attention to the titles. What a wrong thing for me to allow. This guy ended up moving more than just his books in. He kept bringing more and more of his belongings to my place until he had virtually moved in with me. No, I was not okay with it. I wasn't even attracted to him.

At one point, he suggested we try communal living with his family. This guy ended up being into so much into occult involvement it almost made my head hurt. He was completely working for the dark side. At one point, he even told me that he had completely souled his soul to the devil and he would never serve God. When I said no to communal living and all of his "invitations" to join the dark side, he began to put "special seasonings" and poison into my food, but they did not work. God continued to protect me even though I was naïve to the tactics of the devil.

When he tried to convince me that my Jesus was only a Prophet and not the Messiah, I knew I had to get this man out of my house. Sometimes, he would get so mad at me, I wondered how I would survive until I could somehow get him to leave. The times of me listening to my Bible Stories as a kid helped me keep the lies from taking root in my spirit. I now know this is one of the main tactics of the devil. He brings confusion into our minds and tries to get us to buy into his lies.

In John 10:10, Jesus warns us, "The thief does not come except to steal, and to kill, and to destroy. I have come that they may have life and that they may have it more abundantly."

Finally, I told him my mother was coming to town to stay with me and I needed him to leave. We told him if he didn't leave, we have to get the authorities involved. After he moved out, he would call and taunt me. I felt like I was going to lose my mind. There is no doubt in my mind I was in the midst of severe spiritual warfare. I was seeing things, hearing things, and feeling things. I suspected he loosed some sort of evil on me. Finally, I prayed. I knew I was in need of a miracle!

I heard the voice of the Lord speak to me from heaven and say, "Dana, go home, Dana go home."

Though I knew I'd had an encounter with evil, after I went home, it took another "encounter" to change my life forever.

After a night of partying with my cousin, we went back to her house. All of a sudden, the room got very cold. I couldn't comprehend what was going on. This was definitely out of the norm. Then my cousin began to speak in a male's voice, calling out to me. I jumped up off of the couch and ran to the kitchen to get the salt to throw over my shoulder. The evil spirit spoke out of her and she started laughing in a very evil way.

My cousin was possessed and asked me, "Dana, do you want to make a deal with the devil? You can have anything you want."

I yelled, "No! I will never make a deal with the devil!"

Then I ran out of the house and closed myself in a payphone booth. She followed me outside and kept taunting me. A car suddenly came out of nowhere at 3:00 a.m. with three guys in it. Running to the street, I desperately flagged down the car and asked them if they would take me home. As I got in the car, my cousin pushed her way in as well. She kept going in and out as the evil spirit kept trying to take over. I told the three guys she had an evil spirit and not to listen to her.

When she began to call out their birthdays, one of the guys asked, "Should we do an exorcism?"

Scared out of my wits, the only verse I could think of was the 23rd Psalm, so I spoke it out loud all the way to my friend's house. "Yea, though I walk through the valley of the shadow of death, I will fear no evil; for You are with me; Your rod and Your staff, they confront me."

When we got to my friend's house, I jumped out of the car and ran into the house. My cousin's hair was standing straight up on top of her head. She looked like a crazy woman as she ran after me, calling out my name.

I locked her out, but she kept running around the outside the house and yelling, "Dana, come out. I want you so bad, but I can't touch you."

Overwhelmed with fear, I didn't sleep a wink all night. All I could think of was going to church the next morning. My childhood foundation reminded me that was the safest place I could be. I had so much opposition the next morning trying to get to church, but I got there.

My Life Changes Forever

I was able to speak with the Pastor briefly before service about what had happened to me the previous night.

He told me, "You met the devil last night. Go in and enjoy the service. Afterward, we will talk and then we will go see about your cousin."

He preached about my whole life that morning. It was like he had read my diary. I gave my life to the Lord that day. Jesus spoke to me through one of His prophetesses. His peace was like ocean waves washing over me.

His message to me through His prophetess was, "Dana, don't ever go back."

My life radically changed, and I have never been the same. That night, I had a dream about the guys that picked me up that night when the devil spoke through my cousin. In my dream, they said, "Hello, Sister Dana." I was so excited to be called Sister Dana. They looked at each other and said, "She doesn't remember us."

Right after that, I woke up. I clearly recalled the dream and said, "They were angels sent by God!"

Knowing God had sent me to that church, I sat under that Pastor and was trained, equipped, and anointed for service to the kingdom. All I enjoyed doing was going to church, fasting, praying, and worshipping God. He gave me some new friends, too.

Call to Ministry

Right before I accepted my call into the ministry, I got very sick. I went from doctor to doctor trying to find out what was wrong with me. None of them seemed to be able to diagnose the problem. I prayed. After I told my Pastor I couldn't go forth with ministry because of this autoimmune disease, he began to pray for me as well.

God visited me and told me that if I harken unto His Word, He would heal me. I began standing on the Word of God for complete healing.

One day on the way to church, the Spirit of God came into my car like a mighty rushing wind. The presence of God was so strong I had to pull over and get out the car and praise Him.

He spoke to me and said I was going to preach the gospel of Jesus Christ. I got back in the car and went to church. I was so shocked, I ran inside, got on my knees, and told the Lord, "Yes, Lord, I will answer Your call."

I couldn't use the excuse that I was a woman or that no one would want to listen to me because of my past. I began preaching shortly after that and saw many come to know His amazing grace through my testimony.

A short time later, I met a great man of God, Pastor Anthony N. Williams. He came to my church with his mother all the way from Florida to support and lead praise and worship for a Bishop out of Georgia who came to minister at our church. His best friend was an Elder at my church and had invited him. It pays to be in the right place at the right time. He got my number from my Pastor's wife and he called me.

We visited, got to know each other, and dated for two years before we got married. Our wedding was a true blessing. So many people blessed us for our big day. We had very little out of pocket expenses to pay. Our honeymoon was also gifted and taken care of by loving friends and family. God had a plan for us as husband and wife.

After faithfully serving in my husband's local church, God called him to pastor his own church. In 2005, my husband and I planted a ministry in DeLand, Florida. We have been blessed this year with fourteen years of ministry and nineteen years of marriage so far. We have seen miracles, signs, and wonders performed. Our ministry has even gone to Jamaica to host a health fair along with sharing the Word of God.

One of my husband's brother's and his girlfriend got into some trouble and we had the opportunity to take custody of their kids. We were able to nurture and provide a stable home for these precious children until their parents could take over raising them again. The kids are now doing great in school and prospering. His brother is doing well now, too! Our God is so faithful.

In my closing, I want to encourage anyone who may be going through sickness, pain, or trials to not give up on God. In 2013, I had a major setback in my health, but I cried out to God and right there in my room, I experienced the presence of God. He encouraged me to never give up and that I was healed. It reminded me of the story in Matthew 9:1-8 of the paralyzed man whose friends laid him at the feet of Jesus. When Jesus told the man to pick up his bed and walk, the man did what Jesus had instructed him to do.

When I got up from the floor, there was a feather laying under my stomach. I kept asking, "How did that get there?" It was like no other feather I had ever seen in my life. It was spiral at the top. I regret that I threw it away. Later, I saw on a Christian program the same type of feather that I had in my presence. It was a gift that was left by an angel. God sent His special messenger to bring His healing to me.

God will use various ways to accomplish His purpose in your life.

Don't give up on God. He is your healer and it is well with your soul.

Jesus is saying to you today, "Son or Daughter, your faith has made you well. Go in peace and be healed of your affliction. Now, go and do what I have called and equipped you to do."

ABOUT DANA WILLIAMS

Dana R. Williams, a native of Spartanburg, South Carolina, and Leland, North Carolina, is a published author of a book entitled, "Oh How I Love to Dance." Together with her husband Pastor Anthony Williams, Dana Williams serves as pastor of New Life International Ministries in Deland, Florida. She was called into the ministry over nineteen years ago and is dedicated to leading women to the throne of grace through prayer and counseling. In 2014, the Lord birthed a Women's Ministry within her called Jewels of Faith, to empower women and teen girls to go forth in their calling.

LINDA OPPERMAN

GOD PREPARES HIS FRIENDS FOR THE PITS OF PRESSURE

BY LINDA OPPERMAN

Beginning in January of 1984, the Lord started waking me up daily at 4:30 a.m. to spend two hours with Him in prayer. This went on until our plane crash occurred. The Lord was preparing me for what was coming. What God speaks in the pasture of peace we are able to apply in the pits of pressure. On January 12, 1984, God gave me a verse. I wasn't certain why, but later I knew the reason. It was taken from Psalm 118:17, "I shall not die but live that I may glorify the works of the Lord."

My journey with the Lord began at a very early age. I've always had a love and reverence for God. I was born into a Roman Catholic household. There was even a monsieur and nun in the family. When I was two years old, I became very sick. The doctors were perplexed. Eventually, my mother found a doctor in Santa Fe, New Mexico who diagnosed me with tuberculosis. Come to find out a man with tuberculosis had died in the bedroom I occupied. To make matters worse, my friend's home where I played had an active case of TB.

When my relatives learned of my illness and diagnosis, they began to pray for my life. Due to their beliefs, they would light candles and pray to the Holy Trinity as well as many saints. The TB had taken my left lung and was moving to my stomach. My doctor wanted to send me to Arizona to a sanitarium for healing. Due to my age, my parents kept me at home and moved my grandmother in to nurse me.

God healed me from tuberculosis! I didn't realize that until I was a freshman at the University of New Mexico at Albuquerque. I was nineteen years old at the time when I went for my annual lung x-ray; a requirement by doctors ever since I'd become ill. The radiologist this particular year asked why I was there. I explained my bout with TB as a two-year-old.

The doctor replied, "I don't understand? Once the lungs are scarred, they are scarred for life."

He asked me to come and view my x-rays.

"Look you have no scars!" he pointed out.

As I drove back to college, the Holy Spirit spoke these words to my heart, "Though your relatives were praying to the saints for their lack of understanding, their prayers reached the throne of God. You no longer have lung scars because my Son carries the scars for you."

Throughout the years, God has intervened numerous times to spare my life. Once, I was studying at the UNM campus library. There was news of a rapist on campus. All the girls were required to have an escort as we made our way to class. One day, I was on the third floor of the library when it turned dark before I knew it. I felt an awareness of a man filing books on the shelf near me. There was this uneasy feeling. The Lord impressed upon my heart to leave. The uneasy feeling was profound, so I inquired of the librarian at the main desk to ask about the man filing books. The librarian said no one is filing books now. She asked me to take her to the location. Apparently, the books were filed incorrectly. The man used the books as a ploy to be near me.

The next day, I was in speech class and two Albuquerque policemen came to pull me from class. They took me to headquarters to identify the rapist from a line-up, as they believed I had seen him the night before in the library. I looked at the lineup, however, I did not see him. The Lord had protected me.

Eventually, my high school sweetheart proposed I marry him

before he shipped out to an Army base in West Germany. We married and lived abroad for a few years. When we returned to the United States, my husband Hal worked for Trans-world Airlines (TWA) in an entry-level job. By the '80s, Hal had moved up to mid-level management with TWA. It was the Reagan years and President Reagan had laid off air traffic controllers. Hal and I had always felt a calling to ministry. It was during this time an opportunity opened for Hal to enter full-time ministry in Las Vegas, Nevada. In August of 1983, we were offered a job to serve as an associate pastor with a dear friend in Lubbock, Texas. A Word was given to us by our friend saying, "There is a great and effectual door waiting for you, but there are many adversaries." Little did I know what fire we would soon enter.

Beginning in January of 1984, the Lord was waking me up to spend quality time with him at 4:30 a.m. each day. I would read the Word, pray, and sit at the Lord's feet for answers and revelations. By April of the same year, the Lord gave me Psalm 118:17 verse, "I shall not die but live that I might glorify the works of the Lord." I wasn't prepared for its meaning nor did I understand it at the time, but I did date it in my Bible.

Hal had a private pilot's license and had access to a Beechcraft single-engine plane. Many times, he'd fly the pastoral staff to church retreats. On May 4, 1984, Hal was to fly three of us to a weekend retreat in Ruidoso, New Mexico. I didn't love flying in small planes. Due to my anxiety, I actually made a hand-written will the night before making provisions for our two daughters. Off we flew from Lubbock, Texas to Ruidoso, New Mexico with my girlfriend, Ron the senior pastor, Hal, and myself.

Ruidoso had a small airport with a landing trip tucked in a flat area at the bottom of a bowl of mountains. Normally, if an attempt to land is difficult the pilot will circle back around for a re-attempted landing. It was an exceptionally windy day with 40 mph winds. Hal nearly touched down, but our plane kept swerving toward a row of parked planes. After aborting that landing, Hal called the tower and made a re-approach. We never heard back from the tower. This airport was different. Instead of circling back, it would have been better to fly straight through and out of the bowl of mountains. Hal banked right to see pine tree. He banked left to again see mountains and pine trees. The last-ditch effort was to climb up out of the bowl of mountains, but by this point, we lost lift.

My husband said, "We're not going to make it."

I was the only one in the cockpit that didn't hear him say that. Our Senior Pastor who sat adjacent to Hal, who had spoken a Word over us years earlier, turned back to look at me and pray aloud. At that point, I joined him in prayer without knowing why. As the plane went down, we collided with a tree with force causing the plane's front to cave in and the tree to snap. The plane was forced into another nearby tree with the tail being caught on a branch, this left the plane at an angle where the front of the plane was on the ground and the tail facing the sky. I never lost consciousness, nor did I feel pain. The engine came through the cockpit killing our pastor. His chair came back to hit me, resulting in twelve compound fractures, a seatbelt tear to my abdomen, and a crushed skull hemorrhaging the right lobe of my brain. I was struggling to get up when my friend next to me told me I'd been hurt and to stay still. It puzzled me that I saw some workers standing 10 feet from the plane. They would not come to us or respond to our cries for help. I looked out my window and saw aviation fuel gushing down the side of the plane. I never thought of fire or death. I assumed we were waiting on the fire department to arrive and hose down the wreckage.

The jaws of life broke me free of the wreckage. I don't recall very much from that point on, but learned I was transported to the Rio Hondo Hospital where they felt inept to help me, so they transferred me by police escort to Roswell, New Mexico. I needed a neurosurgeon and Roswell had one. Apparently, I was left in the emergency room for 3 hours awaiting the proper staff, but also to see if I might die. Doctors believed I would never be normal again due to the severity of injuries and my exposed brain. The reason I know this is my first cousin happened to be the photographer from the scene for the local newspaper.

I didn't die, so the hospital called eleven doctors back on duty.

The surgeons worked elbow to elbow on my five-foot frame, putting bones back in place, repairing my intestines from a seatbelt rupture, and closed my scalp with metal staples. Although the surgery was successful, I did end up losing most of my frontal lobe. The prognosis was for me to be in a wheelchair my entire life, with limited mental abilities.

Later we learned our church and family were praying for intervention which God honored. I spent a month in ICU at St. Mary's Hospital, Roswell, New Mexico, connected to life support for a time. They brought my parents into the room and I tried to smile. My right eye was stapled shut due to the front brain surgery.

The doctors said, "Bring the daughters in to see how she reacts."

My oldest daughter Lisa was fifteen and my younger daughter Lori was thirteen. They were escorted into the ER and tears came down my face. The doctors were elated because my tears meant I had memories and knew my girls. This meant the brain surgery was a success.

During this one month in the hospital in New Mexico, I encountered a nurse that was cruel to me. She would wait for my parents to go to dinner so she could enter the room to harass me. I recall she came into my room with plyers for cutting plaster casts.

She shoved them in front of my face saying, "You are so ugly, you never smile, I should pinch your nose off."

At that point, she was called out of my room by a head nurse and I recall crying and asking God, "Why does this woman hate me so?"

The answer that came to my spirit said, "Light met darkness."

When you are at your weakest the enemy of your soul tries his hardest to take you out. During this time in my life, I had to censor everything coming into my mind. Was it of God, was it the brain surgery, or was it the enemy? Since this was a Catholic hospital, the Catholic priest on staff and two nuns prayed by my bed daily to encourage me.

I heard a statement once that God does not give dying grace on non-dying days. However, when you are that close to death, His presence is immense. I did experience two visions of heaven that involved the pastor that was killed in the crash. God is so faithful to walk with you through the fire, which is one of my favorite scriptures, Isaiah 43:1-2.

> *Fear not: for I have created you, I have called you*
> *by name, you are mine. When you pass*
> *through the waters, I will be with you; and*
> *through the rivers, they shall not overflow you.*
> *When you walk through the fire, you shall not*
> *be burned; neither shall the flame kindle*
> *upon you.*

For fifteen days, no one told me Pastor Ron Wahlrobe had been killed. He was like a brother to me and Hal. The doctors came in my room one morning to say I had an ulcer now that they would prescribe medication for it. At that time, they told me I could not survive one more thing going wrong with my body. In other words, they were asking me to search my heart to find what I was so concerned with. That night, God in His mercy, transported me from my hospital bed to a large room with books in heaven. The room had windows, but no glass and brightness that filled the room. I stood next to Jesus observing people reading many books. I did not see our Lord face to face, but I knew it was Him next to me, dressed in royalty with colors of purple, gold, and white. As I looked down an aisle of books, I saw Pastor Ron with his arms full of books. I'll never forget the smile upon his face. He was so happy. The Lord and I were observing him, but Ron could not see us. s Pastor Ron headed to a table, I bent passed the Lord to see where Ron was going. I felt a tap on my shoulder.

The Lord said, "Why are you worried about Ron? He's in glory."

At that instant, I was back in my hospital bed. The only limb I could move was my left arm.

I raised it to the ceiling and cried out to the Lord, "Thank You for showing me where Ron is. I knew he was there but thank You because now I can release him."

Due to this vision, I released Ron Wahlrobe and the doctors were able to take me off of ulcer medication.

Being a friend of God isn't just for now; being God's friend is for eternity. God is reaching out to you and desires to become your Best Friend Forever. Befriend God!

About Linda Opperman

Hal and Linda Opperman were leaders at Trinity Church in the '90s and went through a near-death plan crash in which their pastor perished as shared in this testimony by Linda. Hal was on staff as Church Administrator. In the 2000s, Hal and Linda lived in Las Vegas where they were active lay leaders in their church and Hal consulted with churches in building fund campaigns. After Hal's passing, Linda continued to live and minister in Las Vegas and share her testimony of God's healing power and grace wherever she went.

PASTOR DAVID GARCIA

GOD'S FRIEND HAS BEEN
DELIVERED FROM ADULTERY
& DEMONS!

-PASTOR DAVID GARCIA

My name is David Garcia. I was born and raised in New York City and I grew up in a housing project in the '50s and '60s. My testimony is that Jesus Christ delivered me from self-righteousness, adultery, and demon oppression. The amazing thing is that I got saved in a hotel room by myself. I had an experience sort of like the apostle Paul when he got knocked off his horse on the road to Damascus. I don't recall anybody ever sharing the Gospel with me, so God chose to save me in a very different way.

I had good hard-working parents and we were nominal Catholics. My dad worked as a guard in the US Post Office in Grand Central Station. At that time, they would carry guns to protect the Post Office which had a lot of money. My mother was a seamstress. I was what they would call a latch-key kid before the term ever came out. After school, my older brother and I would go home in the projects where a neighbor would take care of us until my parents got home. My mother would leave a list of chores for us to do and our parents would come home after 5 p.m. We were raised with old fashioned values to work hard and do good in school.

My mother is Chinese Cuban and my father Puerto Rican. I never met my paternal grandparents, but in June and July of 1958, we went to Havana, Cuba, to visit my maternal grandparents. I tried to communicate with my grandparents, but for most of our visit, my brother and I would play outside. While I was there, an adult man molested me and then made me watch his parents in the act of sex. From that point on, a spirit of lust gained a very powerful grip on me and dominated my life. I was introduced to a world of adulthood that no child should be exposed to right before I turned nine years old. I also developed a hatred towards the man who did this to me.

This was a time when children were seen and not heard. I told my parents, but it was hushed up. I never went to counseling. I would have extreme nightmares. When I came back to the States, I turned nine years old and resumed elementary school in September of 1958. I began to fantasize with girls. Often, I would bump into girls to touch them. I remember having a very strong lust. It was a demonic stronghold.

At night, I would dream of doing violence to the man that did this to me. I would fantasize that one day I was going to get even. So, not only did I have a strong spirit of lust, but I also had bitterness and unforgiveness towards this man. All through high school, I battled lust. I went on dates with young women and engaged in heavy making out. I graduated from high school in June of 1968. The Vietnam War was going on, but because I attended college, and had a previous knee injury, I had a draft deferment and was not drafted. At that time, I had a full-time job and a full-time girlfriend. I dropped out of college in November of 1970 and began working in the South Bronx as a community worker, helping people solve housing problems, and working in drug education with school students. I always had a good job.

At this time, I became fascinated with the Ouija Board and became intrigued with "speaking to spirits of the dead." My father was a Free Mason at the time. I don't know if you know this, but the Free Mason symbol is G for "God." However, saying you believe in "God" can mean something other than the true God of the Bible. If you are part of the Free Masons, get out because it will cause you to be demon oppressed and bring oppression to your family.

My dad being a Free Mason, one day took me to a spiritualist church with him to listen to a person giving lectures and simultaneously do mind-reading of some of the people in attendance. I became fascinated with spiritism, particularly speaking to the dead which the Bible calls necromancing. I scheduled a private meeting with a spiritualist. I was amazed because familiar spirits began to tell me all kinds of things as if my ancestors were talking to me. It was fascinating, but I did not know that it was all demonic and forbidden by God's Word. I didn't know that Deuteronomy 18:9-14 forbids anyone to communicate with the dead, participate in divination (speaking with the spirits of dead people), and to stay away from familiar spirits (demons who know your family and can imitate them).

After that meeting with the spiritualist, I also began "talking to the dead" myself. I would even guess what gifts my friends would bring me, but here's the clincher: I couldn't sleep without having nightmares. Maybe three times a week, I would dream of falling off a cliff and break into thousands of pieces in my nightmare. I would wake up screaming and in cold sweats. If it wasn't demons, it was lust or my own self-righteousness, and I couldn't get out of it. I grew up Roman Catholic, so I prayed the "Our Father" and the "Hail Mary," but that didn't help. I did not know Jesus as my Lord and Savior and had never read the Bible, so I suffered vehemently with nightmares and lust from age eight to age twenty-four when I got saved.

I began dating Nellie in 1971. She was nineteen and I was twenty-one. I soon decided she would be my future wife and that my relationship with her would lead me to Christ. Nellie's maternal grandmother had often taken her to a Spanish speaking Pentecostal church when she was younger. In fact, I even went with her to another Spanish Pentecostal church for a season. They were great and loving people, but in my bondage, I never heard or received the Gospel message of salvation.

On October 16, 1971, the pastor of that church married us. In the first three years of our marriage, we experienced much strife and conflict. Because of me, my home experienced demonic oppression. Every now and then, although Nellie was not a committed Christian, she would pray in Jesus' name. Then we had temporary peace until I started up again with the Ouija Board and listening to demonic spirits.

In 1971, I got a job with a subcontractor to the US Department of Labor. I would get people jobs as apprentices in the building construction industry. I would teach people to pass tests so that they could get jobs as a steamfitter, sheet metal worker, electrician, carpenter, or ironworker. These were very good-paying jobs. From 1972-1974, my assignment was specifically to recruit and train prospective apprentices in the elevator and escalator industry. I traveled to about thirty cities during this time. I had an expense account, a credit card, and my specific task was to recruit and train minority men to pass the union entrance test for the elevator and escalator industry.

While I was traveling, God began to do a work in my life. My wife's maternal grandmother, the one who took her to church as a child, was a quiet but powerful prayer warrior, and would constantly pray for God to save me. We often visited her and she would gently tell me how God was going to use me one day. She didn't preach to me, but lived a godly life in front of me and sweetly exhorted me on how God had great things for me. I respected her, but quietly laughed at that thought. Things began to happen from 1973 onwards.

First of all, on three separate occasions, God spared me from tragedy. One time while in Denver, Colorado, I was trying to have an affair with a Mexican girl in front of a group of Chicano young men. It vehemently angered them that a Puerto Rican guy would do that. They threatened me and I prayed that God would get me out of there in one piece and He did. Another time, I was in Atlanta, Georgia, flirting with two young women at the same time when their boyfriends came home. I was very intoxicated with marijuana at the time and very incoherent, but I knew enough again to ask God to get me out of there unscathed. I remember driving while extremely high and swerving in and out of traffic, simultaneously asking God to get me safely to my hotel room, promising, like the time in Denver, that I would serve Him if He did. On both occasions, I made it back safely, but sadly I chose to go back to a lifestyle of lust, spiritism, and self-righteousness.

≈

In February of 1974, I went to New Orleans to do elevator business, but also to attend the very ungodly Mardi Gras festivities. On the very first night, as I was determined to sin, I felt a tap on my shoulder. When I turned around, a young teenage freckle-faced girl from Teen Challenge, Oklahoma City, said to me, "Sir, you need to read this." She handed me a Gospel tract newspaper that said, "Millions missing after the Rapture!" The tract scared me so much, I got on the first flight out of New Orleans and flew home! The seed of the Rapture had been planted.

The Rapture is a prophesied event in 1 Thessalonians 4:16-17, in which Jesus suddenly comes and snatches or raptures the born-again believers from this world into the air to be with Him forever. It says, "For the Lord Himself will descend from Heaven with a shout, with the voice of an archangel, and with the trumpet of God. And the dead in Christ will rise first. Then we who are alive and remain, will be caught up (raptured) together with them in the air. And this we shall always be with the Lord."

Now my favorite hotel was the Days Inn because my per diem from the government was more than the rate I would pay there and I would pocket the difference, which you weren't supposed to do. One day, my business took me to Tampa, Florida, to work with the elevator contractors and potential apprentices. I was the type, when I arrived in the room, would always draw the curtains closed, put the TV on loudly, and then put the "do not disturb" sign on the outside doorknob. I was a paranoid New Yorker determined I was not going to be robbed or ripped off in Tampa.

Well, I did not know that the owner of the Days Inn was Cecil Day, a born-again Christian, who had Christian book racks in the hotel lobbies for sale. I began to look at them and there was one book in particular that grabbed my attention called, "The Angels Of Light" by Hobart Freeman. On the cover, it said, "ESP, Yoga, talking to the dead...is this God or Satan?" I became incensed. I said, "The nerve of this man saying that this is Satan!" So, I bought the book.

I remember calling my wife around 8 p.m. that evening, saying, "Honey, I have a book by this blankety-blank preacher and I'm going to read it and tell him off! The nerve of this guy saying horoscopes are wrong and talking to the dead is demonic. That's something I do and I believe in."

I was harsh with her, but she gently encouraged me just to read what the book said. I decided I would start to read the next night after business. In the morning, as I was about to leave my room, I started to close the curtains and put on the TV as usual. I heard a voice telling me, "David, why don't you leave your curtains open; don't turn on the TV and put the 'please make my room sign' on the outside of the door."

So, I said, this must be my "spirit guide" talking to me. That night, sure enough, my room was done, with fresh sheets and towels. That night, I started reading a book a fellow worker had given me, "The Late Great Planet Earth" by Hal Lindsey, which talked about "The Rapture." At the same time, I picked up the book which upset me, The Angels of Light, which had spoken against ESP, Karate (which I was into), horoscopes, and talking to the dead. While reading, all hell broke loose. I was sweating profusely. It felt as if the bed was going up and down banging on the floor. Whether this was real or in my mind, I'm not sure but it felt real. My lamp was going on and off. Again, whether this was real or in my mind, I'm not sure, but it seemed so real. I was too scared to continue the book and too scared to put it down.

Then it came to the scripture Deuteronomy 18:9-12 (I was a nominal Catholic, so I had never read a Bible). Deuteronomy 18:9-12 says, "When you come into the land which the Lord your God is giving you, you shall not learn to follow the abominations of those nations. There shall not be found among you anyone who makes his son or his daughter pass through the fire, or one who practices witch-craft, or a soothsayer, or one who interprets omens, or a sorcerer, or one who conjures up spells, or a medium, or a spiritualist, or one who calls up the dead. For all who do these things are an abomina-tion to the Lord, and because of these abominations the Lord your God drives them out from before you."

All of a sudden I said, "My God, I'm going to Hell. I need to stop this."

I wanted to pray so bad but didn't know how. Then I felt to look at "The Late Great Planet Earth" again and Hal Lindsey talked about being born-again. He referred to John 3:16 in the Bible, "For God so loved the world that He gave His only begotten Son, that whoever believes in Him, should not perish but have everlasting life." I wanted everlasting life and decided to read all of John Chapter Three. Thank God there was a Gideon Bible in the room and it referred to the page where John 3:16 could be found. I read all of John chapter three and realized that I needed to be born-again. At this point, I was desperate because I felt the bed banging and the lamp going on and off and a choking feeling.

I cried out and said, "Jesus, I want to be born-again." I got on my knees and began to pray, "Our Father who art in Heaven, hallowed be thy name. Thy kingdom come..." but that didn't work. I said, "Hail Mary full of grace..." but it got worse. I even prayed, "Hail Holy Queen..." but that didn't work.

I was about to pray the Act of Contrition as I learned in the Catholic Church when all of a sudden, a wonderful voice came to me and said, "David, just like you opened the curtains to your room and put 'please make the room' sign on your door, I want you to open the curtains to your heart and invite Me in. I'll give you new sheets and new towels and I'll clean your life and I'll use you." I tell you, I got on my knees and said, "Jesus, please forgive me for being an adulterer. Please forgive me for talking to the dead. I didn't know it was witch-craft. I open the curtains to my heart, and I want You to come in and give me new sheets and towels and use me."

All of a sudden, a load lifted and I had no more choking feelings. I felt clean and that the power of lust and witchcraft lifted from me. I had total peace for the first time in twenty years. It was three in the morning and I called Nellie to tell her what had happened. I decided to take the first flight out in the morning. I told my boss I needed three days off (so that I could read the New Testament in my Gideon Bible which the hotel gave to me). Over the next three days, I read the whole New Testament. I had relied on Nellie to answer any of my questions as she was more familiar with the Bible than I was. We then saw Billy Graham preaching on television and said the sinners' prayer as a couple.

In May of 1974, a friend named Carmen invited us to her church. We went to an Assembly Of God church pastored by a born-again Jewish man named Jerry. He was beginning a series on Jesus is L-O-R-D, using each letter to describe Jesus. That day he spoke on Jesus is Love and it impacted both of us so much, we made our way to the altar to fully commit our lives to Jesus.

We became involved in the church ministries and gradually grew in the Lord. We taught Sunday School, were involved in Men's and Women's ministries, and in Street Evangelism. In 1975, we became involved with Children's and Youth ministries.

In January of 1976, I left my very good paying job as a subcontractor to the US Department Of Labor to work full time at our church as missionaries with no salary but a small stipend. Our job was to clean the church, do minor repairs, and do Street Evangelism. We worked from January of 1976 until July of 1980. At the invitation of a friend named David, we planned to go to Rhodesia, in Southern Africa. Well, to make a long story short, in July of 1980, we left as missionaries to Zimbabwe, the new name of the country. First, we worked for the Pentecostal Assemblies of Canada from '80 to '81. Then we planted a church in a city called Mutare and pastored it for two years. It was only the second multi-racial church at that time in the country. We then took over a Bible School in Harare for 18 months.

In November of 1984, God had made it clear that we were to return to America. We had no idea where we would wind up, but "faithful is He who calls you who also will do it." We wound up in a wonderful Charismatic church in Edmond, Oklahoma, where I established credentials with the Assemblies of God. We began to send out resumes and in March of 1985, we took over First Assembly of God, Gallup, New Mexico, where we had a fast-growing, multi-ethnic church consisting of Anglos, Native Americans, and Mexican Americans. After three and a half years of successful ministry, we felt the call to Florida and took over the pastorate of the then Brooksville Assembly of God, forty-five miles north of Tampa. There, the church experienced steady growth; three building programs (all debt-free) with many saved, discipled, and called to ministry. Nellie and I were there thirty years, from May of 1988 to May of 2018. After reading a book by Michael Brown, "How Saved Are We," I felt God was calling me to "Save the saved" as Dr. Brown had put it in his book.

For the last year, 2018-2019, we've been traveling and ministering all over the US and some other countries. Our ministry is called, Ministry 128, after Colossians 1:28, "Him we preach, warning every man and teaching every man in all wisdom, that we may present every man perfect in Christ Jesus."

We graciously have been seeing a move of God wherever we go. Hundreds of souls saved, deliverances, some healings, and a deep cry for holiness and righteousness.

We serve a wonderful God and He's coming back very soon. I encourage you to fully surrender your life to Jesus Christ. Make sure you are not a lukewarm Christian and that you have not "left your first love" (Revelation 2:4-5). Make sure that you repent of all known sins. Get into a Bible-preaching church. Leave your sinful life and do not be dominated by your old nature. Don't be fooled: Jesus is coming back for a church without spot or wrinkle (Ephesians 5:27). He will help you through the power of the Holy Spirit to live for Him and serve Him. If Jesus can take an adulterer, a self-righteous person involved in spiritism like me, and save me, He'll save and use you.

I'm going to give you an example of a sinner's prayer, so if you are not a thousand percent sure that you're going to Heaven; if you're not born-again, please pray this prayer:

> Lord Jesus Christ, I come to You right now by faith. I realize I'm a sinner. I have done things that are spoken against in Your Word, the Bible. Please forgive me. I believe and confess that Jesus, You are the Son of God and You shed Your innocent blood for all my sins on the cross of Calvary. I repent of all my sins. Wash me in Your blood and take away my sins. Nail them to the cross. Jesus, I also confess and believe that You were resurrected on the third day. You are alive. You defeated death and sin and because You live, take over my life right now. I receive You as my Lord and Savior. Jesus, put me in a Bible-preaching church where I'm going to hear the truth, grow in the knowledge and grace of Your Word, and I'll serve You the rest of my life. I thank You for saving me today. In Jesus' name, I pray, Amen.

Now, I bless you in the name of Jesus. I bless you right now that you will be free from all your iniquity, all your flesh, all the curses in your life are broken right now in the name of Jesus! I speak blessings on you that you will be set free by the power and grace of God from every stronghold of Satan. That you will go on to live a fruitful life, put on the fruit of the Spirit, the whole armor of God, and live a successful, victorious Christian life. I decree all of this over you, in Jesus' name. Amen.

About David Garcia

*David A. Garcia has served as Lead Pastor of **Grace World Outreach Church**, Brooksville, Florida, since 1986. Under his leadership, the 2300 plus seat Grace Dome was built and completed in 2.5 years totally debt free!*

David travels throughout America preaching and conducting Revivals and Deeper Life teachings. He serves as advisor and spiritual father to several pastors. Also, David conducts purity conferences for men and women, as well as purity and dating seminars for students and millennials. Additionally, David has authored four books; Don't Awaken Love Before it's Time, Redefining Sex & Dating, The Powerful Last-Day Christian and The Gospel of the Kingdom of God.

David and his wife Nellie have been married 47 years and have two happily married children, both serving God as Pastors and four wonderful grandchildren.

ALLEN EARLS

OVERCOMING OBSTACLES AS A FRIEND OF GOD

ALLEN EARLS

How do you go from being very poor, with four sisters and a brother, living in a two-bedroom house with no indoor plumbing, no central heat or air conditioning, and no telephone, to something extraordinarily better? What if you also had an alcoholic father with violent tendencies? How do you go from those difficult circumstances to being in Senior Management for some of America's largest companies, to obtaining principal roles in major motion pictures and television shows, and traveling around the world, seeing the beautiful earth God created?

My story begins growing up in the North Georgia mountains with my four older sisters: Sandra, Hazel, Claudine, and Sherry, and my older brother, William, living in a broken-down house we called home. Although there were a lot of serious problems and struggles within my family, my mother, Eva Mae Earls, was an extraordinary woman who was smart and faithful to God. She laid a spiritual foundation for me that was the beginning of my spiritual journey. Over time, it would transform my life forever as I walked through the phases of becoming a friend of God.

Phase I – Becoming a Born-Again Believer

Although my mother took me to church regularly as a child, the process of transforming my life really began in earnest when I became a born-again believer at approximately fourteen years of age. This happened when I simply asked God for His forgiveness, declared I believed in His Son Jesus Christ, that He died on the cross for my sins, was raised from dead on the third day, and asked Him to come into my heart. Becoming a born-again believer activated the covenant of grace in my life wherein everything God promised in His Word He was now obligated to fulfill for me, if only I believed. I held Him to His word by reminding Him of the promises He had made to me in His Word, such as Philippians 4:19, "But my God shall supply all your need according to his riches in glory by Christ Jesus." (NJKV) My coming to the revelation that God wanted me to hold Him accountable to what He said in scripture did not come to me immediately. As I spent time with Him and began to get to know Him personally in this new relationship, I grew as a Christian.

Phase II – Developing the Relationship

I began to nurture my new relationship with God by setting time aside to listen to great Gospel and contemporary Christian music. I would spend at least an hour a week alone with God, listening to and simply singing along with these great artists who were giving God praise. After listening to a few songs, I would spend a few minutes reading the Bible, even though I didn't always fully understand what I was reading. However, the key was that I was spending time with God and getting to know Him.

During this time, I also continued to attend church regularly, attended Bible studies, and tried to have good fellowship with other believers who were on the same journey. As these things were taking place, I was learning more about God and His Word, but more importantly, I was developing an intimate relationship with Him. I was learning He wanted to be a part of everything in my life and began recognizing His voice when He was speaking to me in my spirit. I was becoming His friend.

Phase III – Applying His Word to My Life to Get Results

As my relationship with God grew, I became very close to Him. I enjoyed my quiet time with Him as I got to know Him, asking Him what I should do in certain situations, and just sharing my life with Him. I also learned I could trust Him, that He was "for me" not "against me," and He had a purpose for my life. He was real and wanted to manifest for me everything He had promised in His Word. As different circumstances presented themselves in my life, such as needing clothes, money for daily needs, money for college, a job, etc., I began recalling scriptures that as close as possible referenced these things. I began to remind God of His promises to supply all my needs in His Word and began to put Him to the test to supply those things for me.

As I began to exercise my faith, I learned it didn't matter what the situation looked like, God could and did change the results. I learned to thank God in advance before the thing or situation I was praying for or about occurred. All these things I am sharing with you in this book, I learned over many years, not all at once. However, as I incorporated them into my life, I began to get more and more positive results and I learned how to "win" as a friend of God.

Because you are reading this book, you will benefit from all of my years of experience in learning how to win in life and overcome any obstacle you may face. There are many other important principles you should learn and apply to your life, such as the following ones I discuss in my book, *Secrets from the Spiritual Giants*:

1. Spend time in God's presence with praise and worship.
2. Stand on God's Word for your situation.
3. Pray and fast in the midst of the battle.
4. Forgive and become free to soar.
5. Confess the results you expect.

6. Thank God for success before it happens.

7. Sow to activate seedtime and harvest.

I can't share everything I have learned in this one chapter, but if you do the things I have described in this book, you can overcome poverty or any other challenge and "win" no matter what hand you have been dealt in life.

The Manifestation of Results

Whether it is formal education (i.e., high school, trade school, college, or post-graduate level studies), continuing professional education, informal classes, instructional videos on the internet, or mentoring programs, learn as much information as you can in your area of interest. Include what you are passionate about, your God-given gifts and talents, and what God has ultimately called you to do in life.

Despite my family's poverty, I was a straight "A" student in high school and college because I listened well and studied hard. I also prayed God would help me understand the things I didn't understand, help me remember things I should remember, and help me perform at my best when it was time to take a test. I prepared very well and then I called upon God to do His part in helping me. By faith, I believed He would never let me down and He did not. He will do the same for you.

My family was very poor, so money was always an issue. When I was in high school, I was an athlete who played basketball, football, ran track, and other sports. I wanted to purchase my sports "letter jacket." However, my parents had no money to buy a jacket for me. I prayed about it and asked God to help me obtain the jacket. Soon thereafter, I learned about an essay writing contest at my high school where the winner of the contest would receive a cash prize. At the time, I was not a very good writer. However, I felt the Spirit of God telling me to enter the contest. I clearly did not want to enter the contest, especially since it was open to the entire high school.

After about three weeks of arguing with God about this paper, I finally said, "Okay, God, I will do it only because You are telling me to do it."

I did my best and wrote the paper. A couple of months later, my English teacher indicated there was a winner of the essay contest in our class. She then announced to the class that I had won the contest. I found out afterward that I had won by default because no one else in the entire high school had entered the contest. I used the winning cash to purchase my sports letter jacket.

When God tells you to do something, you just do it!

With God's help and a lot of studying, I graduated from high school third in my class. However, my family had no money to pay for a college education for me. I remembered Philippians 4:19 where God had promised me He would supply my every need according to His riches in glory through Christ Jesus. I prayed and asked God for the money for college. I put my faith into action by applying for every scholarship known to mankind, working three part-time jobs, and becoming a tither on what little money I earned. Thanks be to God, He answered my prayers and I received a lot of small scholarships. After four years of tremendous work and absolute trust in God, I graduated Magna Cum Laude and "Thank-You Lordy" from the University of North Georgia. I now had a Bachelor of Business Administration Degree in Accounting and a minor in Computer Science, with a 3.84 GPA on a 4.00 scale.

Applying God's Word to your life and exercising your faith, always works and gets you results.

After graduation, I was hired by Ernst & Young, one of the world's largest Public Accounting Firms, and you better believe, it was God that helped me soar during the interview process. As I continued to grow in God and in the knowledge of His Son Jesus Christ, I was given clients across multiple industries, obtained a tremendous amount of business experience, passed the CPA Exam, and became a Certified Public Accountant while adding a lot of value to the firm.

After several years and multiple promotions, I decided to leave the firm and go to work for a $10 billion publicly-traded company in the consumer products industry called Georgia-Pacific Corporation.

While I worked at Georgia-Pacific, I continued to grow and learn more about the Word of God and how to apply it to my life. I added a tremendous amount of value to the company and received numerous promotions over the years by continuing to use all of the previously mentioned tools in my spiritual toolbox. At one point in my career, I became eligible for company bonuses. I prayed for bonuses of a minimum of $25,000 per year at the beginning of the year and then spent the entire year thanking God, on a daily basis, for having received the bonuses before they were actually received (Romans 4:17). After several years in a row of performing at a high level on the job and hitting the requested bonus target of a minimum of $25,000, God asked me a question through my spirit.

He first told me He was a God of precision and He had given Noah the precise measurements for building the Ark. Therefore, for the upcoming year, He wanted to know specifically what kind of bonus I wanted versus me continuing to say "a minimum of $25,000."

He said, "Do you want a $26,000 bonus or something else?"

I said, "Okay, God, I'm going to stretch my faith to a place I have never gone before because I trust You and believe in You. As a result, I am asking for and expecting a $40,000 bonus for the upcoming year."

I immediately began to thank God on a daily basis for having already received the $40,000 bonus, even though it had not yet come to pass. During my professional career, I had never in my life received a bonus of this size, but with God, I knew all things were possible if I believed (Mark 9:23). After continuing to perform on the job at a high level and many months of daily thanking God for the $40,000 bonus and declaring I had already received it, the company finally announced the bonuses to eligible employees. Even though there was a downturn in the economy during that year, my boss told me my bonus for the year was $42,000.

To God be the glory for the things He has done!

Just for the record, the purpose for my success and financial increases was not for me to just spend it upon myself. It was for me to be able to help more people through higher giving and to be able to continue to help spread the Gospel of Jesus Christ around the world as I continued to tithe on my income.

Time to Step out of the Boat and onto the Water

After many years of specifically trying to determine my purpose in life, I realized my purpose and "calling" were to use all of my gifts, talents, and the things I was passionate about (i.e., business, music, films, and television, etc.) to help others and to help spread the Gospel of Jesus Christ around the world through non-traditional ways. To that end, after hearing from God in my spirit, I became a partner in a "Christian Night Club," which at the time was a cutting-edge concept for the body of Christ. Jay Glover, his wife Gloria, and I, successfully operated *Club Soteria* for about five years, ministering to people through great gospel music during the weekends.

Also, during my time at Georgia-Pacific, I married my wife Terri Earls, who is very successful in her own right at the highest levels in Corporate America. She is a strong born-again believer impacting the body of Christ in her own way on a daily basis. After my assignment by God at Georgia-Pacific had been fulfilled, God asked me to step out of the boat and walk on the water with Him by asking me to leave the six-figure income at Georgia-Pacific. He had a new adventure planned for me which included being involved in films and television shows. I trusted God, left Georgia-Pacific by faith (with no safety net), and after a few ups and downs, eventually walked on to a major motion picture set as an Extra. With no experience, I began another professional journey with God leading the way. I took the money I earned from that first job as an Extra and sowed all of it back into the Kingdom of God as a first fruit offering (Proverbs 3:9-10).

God has been true to His Word in Proverbs.

I subsequently obtained professional training for becoming a professional actor in Film and Television, and through working hard at my craft and aggressively exercising my faith, God opened doors for me. I continued to apply His Word directly to my life, so my major motion picture credits as a professional actor include one of my favorite films: Tyler Perry's comedy, *Madea Goes to Jail*, which at the time of its release, was the number one movie in America. My latest major motion picture credit, which I am very excited about, is for a principal role in a major blockbuster Disney Movie expected to be released late in 2019. My credits also include co-starring roles as Judge Barlow on the hit Lifetime Television Network TV show, "Drop Dead Diva," as well as National Television Commercials for companies such as Floor and Décor.

By becoming a friend of God through becoming a born-again believer, putting my faith into action, and applying His Word to my life in practical ways, I have overcome poverty and many other great challenges along the way. I continue to give to and help people around the world and I continue to prosper and have great success (Joshua 1:8).

I have also been blessed to see much of this great earth God has created. I have visited Israel, South Africa, China, Italy, France, Switzerland, Ireland, Holland, Mexico, the Bahamas, and Hawaii just to name a few. Further, I continue to have great business success, as I provide Senior Management Leadership to Corporate America and motivate others through Public Speaking. I am also a shareholder in some of the world's largest and most successful companies which include Apple, Inc., Facebook, Twitter, Lyft, Liberty Media, the Atlanta Braves, and Weight Watchers International.

I am a testament to how God can totally transform your life, despite your negative circumstances. If He will do it for me, He will do it for you!

If you would like to overcome poverty or any other challenges in your life and have great success, become a born-again believer, apply His Word to your life, exercise your faith, and incorporate into your life the other previously mentioned principles and nuggets of wisdom. If you do these things, you too will have a positive impact on others, fulfill your God-given calling, and you will win in life! Let's do it together!

If you have questions about how to have success or you want to continue to grow and learn with me on this journey, please send an email to me at earlsent@aol.com. I would love to hear from you. You can follow me on Facebook at Allen Earls and register on my new YouTube channel to be launched in Q1, 2020. I will be launching a new Academy to teach on success principles based on God's Word, so others all over the world can reach the success they desire and become everything God created them to become. Peace and Increase!

ABOUT ALLEN EARLS

Allen Earls is a successful Businessman with more than 20 years of Professional experience. He is a Certified Public Accountant with a proven track record of success in leading professional organizations in some of Corporate America's largest and most profitable companies. He is a successful Entrepreneur, and Professional Actor with Major Network Television Co-Starring role Credits and has Major Motion Picture Credits in some of Hollywood's most notable films. Allen Earls is also a writer, author, prolific public speaker, and highly sought-after success consultant.

DAVID YOUNGREN

A FRIENDSHIP OF LOVE: A STORY OF HEALING AND TRANSFORMATION

BY DAVID YOUNGREN

When I was a teenager attending school in Sweden, I had a teacher who performed a reading experiment with my class. She claimed that one can test a person's ability to read by how many times they move their eyes while reading a line in a book.

"A great reader," she said, "can read an entire line in a book while only moving their eyes once. An average reader can read a line with no more than two movements of their eyes. Anything more than two eye movements is below average."

I made two eye movements of my own in that moment: one nervous look to the student on my right and another anxious glance to the student on my left.

She continued, "Now, open to page 225 in your books. I will go around the room and test each of you individually to observe how many times you shift your eyes to read one line."

Luckily for me, she started at the opposite end of the classroom, making me one of the last students to be examined. I was both excited and nervous. I thought I was smarter than the other students, yet I also struggled with the insecurity that I was not enough.

Holding these two egoic opposites in my mind, I nervously waited for my turn.

By the time the teacher arrived at my desk, all the students had either moved their eyes once or twice. Even the student we ignorantly considered a slow-witted outcast had only moved his eyes twice. I thought to myself, "If he moved his eyes just two times, I'll read it with one movement, no problem."

"Okay, David," she said. "Your turn."

With the teacher's eyes locked onto mine, I stared at the line. How could I keep my eyes from moving? I first considered just staring at the page, but I was too scared I'd get caught, so I read the entire line, hoping that my eyes would not make a single unnecessary movement. Then I looked up. The verdict was about to be announced.

I held my breath, still anticipating that she'd say I read the line in one movement like the "smarter" kids (but I was prepared to settle for a worst-case scenario of two eye movements). She told the class that I had moved my eyes not once, or twice, but three times.

I was devastated. I insisted that something must be wrong, but the teacher would not change her mind. I had scored worse than any other student in the class.

I spent the rest of the day in mourning. Maybe I wasn't a very good reader. Perhaps I wasn't even intelligent. I was in a class for academically gifted students, yet somehow, I no longer felt like I belonged.

It didn't take long for me to forget about the episode. The memory was too painful, so I suppressed it into my subconscious, but as it lodged in there, it had altered my personality and my self-perception. My confidence was replaced with a nagging doubt that I was just not good enough: I was not as gifted or as smart as the other students, so I lost the motivation to study. My grades in every class began to drop. I felt less confident in class and stopped interacting with the other students as I had before. I felt like I was not as good as them, and therefore, I didn't think they would accept me.

Even Success Didn't Satisfy

Many years later, the unconscious memory lived on in my pursuits. Although I was an experienced orator, I would often listen to other well-known speakers and then redesign my message to imitate theirs. I felt that they were smarter than me, so what they had to say was somehow better than my own content. One traumatic moment (or at least one ego-shattering event) had redefined who I believed myself to be. Now, it affected my career and shaped my dreams and pursuits.

By the time I was in my thirties, I was flying high. I'd become the Pastor of a church just outside of Toronto, I was the President of a Bible College, and I traveled the world speaking in large crusades to as many as 100,000 people at the time. I even had my own television show! However, none of it was enough to acquire the acceptance I felt I had to earn.

A combination of guilt, shame, and fear had entrenched itself as the filters through which I viewed reality. I could not be happy with myself even when I did well. It wasn't that the incident in the classroom was the sole reason for my struggles. The unconscious negative programming had begun almost the moment I was born. Somehow, the minor event in the classroom had a traumatic effect on me and intensified the disconnect from unconditional love. Although I was not consciously aware of it, my life was being shaped by one teacher's experiment.

All of us have different experiences that shape our sense of self. We are by-products of our upbringings and what we have experienced and learned in life. Those events live on as the stories we tell ourselves about who we are. Whether our understanding of what happened is factually correct or not doesn't matter, because what remains as an unconscious memory is our interpretation of what happened. Combined with other memories, these stories about who we are, form an egoic pattern in our subconscious that then determines our conscious thought-patterns, beliefs, passions, and pursuits.

Unless we experience transformation, the underlying emotion is fear (whether we are aware of it or not). This fear shows up in a combination of ways, fluctuating from one moment to another as self-doubt or conceit, anxiety or arrogance, self-loathing or self-right-eousness. Lurking below the surface is always an egoic struggle to be unique and superior to others. The inner unconscious anxiety that *I'm not enough* has become part of our identity. Unaware of our true essence—created in the image and likeness of God—we are afraid of rejection and loneliness, scared that our lives won't matter, and worried (or indifferent) about what people think of us. Fear is the unrelenting and unconscious guide of our life.

Excruciating Pain

In 2005, I began to have severe cluster headaches to the point where I felt like someone was sticking a knife in my eye. No matter what I did, including seeking help from doctors and pleading with God to take the pain away, the pain only increased. Even prescribed strong pain killers could not alleviate the pain. I felt hopeless and ready to give up. My religious upbringing made me think that it was God's punishment in my life because inside I felt like a failure who had disappointed God.

Then one day in 2006, I had a deep inner unexplainable prompting to close my eyes and meditate on divine love. It was outside my comfort zone. But there in my car, I closed my eyes and relived with my imagination, the movie, *The Passion of the Christ.* The story of Christ's death communicated the profundity of unselfish, sacrificial, and unconditional love. Suddenly, my imagination turned intimate, and for a moment I felt like I was there...immediately...in the presence of Christ while He carried His cross.

Indescribable love rushed over me.

Within mere moments, the pain subsided. Since then, I have never had another attack of cluster headaches.

A New Understanding of God

Following this dramatic turn of events in my life, my eyes opened to the power of love unlike I had seen before. I found this recurring message of love that transcends all else in many ancient sacred texts.

I found, for instance, in the Bible, a compilation of sixty-six ancient books, a message that my religious background had never really made clear. The Bible was so not so much a history book, although there's much history in there. It was really not a theological discourse with rules to obey, even though I found many rules in there.

It was a story about humanity's quest to understand the purpose of life by interacting with what they perceived to be God, culminating in the revelation of divine love through this mystical human, yet divine figure named Jesus.

The story of the Bible begins with two people in paradise choosing to live by a value system based on adjudicating good from evil. Their choices made them judgmental of themselves and others; their good versus evil binary system caused them to succumb to insecurity and fear. They became disconnected from divine love and enmeshed in selfishness, pride, and fear. They fell from a paradise of love into a hell of separation from each other, their true inner selves, and ultimately from divine love.

The story was metaphorical and mystical because it was more than a story about two people at the beginning of time. It was a story about what happens in the deep areas of our hearts. Insecurity and fear at some point invade our inner person, through judgment of self and others. We become distant and separated from the core essence of our being and from that love that made us innocently enter the dance of life naked without inhibition, fear, and shame.

As the spiritual text continues to unfold, we find how people sought to understand their relationship with whom they believed to be God. They created religious systems and laws, made sacrifices to dull their guilty consciences, and pitted self against others to gain some form of moral superiority. They attempted to quiet the nagging doubt of the false self, the critical voice within that whispered, *"I am not enough."*

Life became a meaningless fight for survival until love took on human form in the person of Jesus, who demonstrated the self-giving and loving nature of the divine. He awakened humanity to the pure love that had been dead inside them. Like the tale of Sleeping Beauty, humans were living in an alternate state, unaware, distant, and separated from their true selves—created to be loved and to love. It took a divine Prince to awaken them to their original design.

With a new understanding of this sacred and revered ancient spiritual text, my life changed. I saw God or whatever name you prefer to use to describe that which transcends all, through a new lens. I began to meditate on this pure love every day.

I knew that what we constantly meditate upon will eventually get in our unconscious mind, leading to a process called *automatization.* Dr. Caroline Leaf, a neuroscientist, explains this process and how it relates to meditation this way:

> *The nonconscious metacognitive mind is filled with the thoughts you have been building since you were in the womb and they form the perpetual base from which you see life (automatization). Up to 99 percent of the decisions you make are based on what you have built and automatized into your nonconscious....*

> — DR. CAROLINE LEAF, SWITCH ON YOUR BRAIN

Dr. Leaf then adds that meditation or imagination changes our subconscious memory and this process of automatization. In other words, what we meditate, imagine, and focus on, eventually becomes part of who we are. It becomes an effortless instinct, natural response, or automatization.

Relating back to my experience, I realized by focusing in meditation on the pure love expressed in a personal (not vague or abstract) way on that historic day 2000 years ago, I was repainting the canvas of my heart. So, I kept directing my emotions and my imagination in meditation until I entered a new state of awareness.

My health suddenly improved drastically. Old crippling attitudes disappeared. Insecurities and fear began to fade. Opportunities effortlessly came my way. Success followed without all its normal pitfalls. I found paradise in me. New dreams emerged from within that would benefit others and make the world a better place.

Lives Transformed by Experiencing the Love of Christ

Then in 2012, I put together a 40-day meditation challenge called *Amazing Life*. Before it was officially published, a friend in the Netherlands asked if I would send it to him for him to preview. At first, I was not eager to share the program because I was concerned about whether it would be accepted, but I emailed him the file of audio downloads anyway. About three weeks later, he excitedly called me and told me of its impact on his life. Within a short period, he had personally involved hundreds of people in the program on several continents. Since then, we have also translated the *Amazing Life* program into Dutch, Spanish, and Swahili. It's now being used in Africa, Europe, Asia, South America, and here in North America as a resource to help people experience the love of Christ.

The reports that I have received from people whose lives have been dramatically impacted by these meditation exercises are beyond anything I could have ever imagined. Whether it was Lois, the woman raised as an orphan, who used the meditations to help her overcome decades of nightly occurrences of nightmares, or Richard from California, who used them to cure many years of insomnia; these simple daily exercises worked for so many because the meditations are designed to heighten awareness of transcending love.

One amazing testimony involves a young mother, Debbie, who after being diagnosed with terminal brain cancer, began practicing the *Amazing Life Meditations*. At first, Debbie was skeptical. As she persisted, she would find herself overwhelmed with the purity and power of love. Six months later, while going through a routine scan of her brain, they discovered that her tumor had dissolved. All the symptoms of cancer had also disappeared. The doctor subsequently gave Debbie a clean bill of health.

So that's my story—my track to embrace the love of Christ. It is forever embedded in my journey of life.

Your life, path story is different, but it is as valid as mine. Whatever your journey of life has been, it is important, significant, and uniquely yours. Although we may or may not share the same beliefs and values, we share our common humanity that deep within cries out for unconditional love. Intuitively, we know that the greatest of all is love. That **love** has the ability to transform us from the inside out and to bear fruits of happiness, peace, and goodness. It's what I call the way of love...

The content and the stories in this chapter have by permission been adapted from the following books by David Youngren:

Awakening To 'I Am Love:' *How Finding Your True Self Transforms Your Wellbeing, Relationships and What You Do* (2019)

Beyond Limits: *7 Steps To Create the Life of Your Dreams* (2016)

ABOUT DAVID YOUNGREN

David Youngren is an international teacher, entrepreneur, author, and philanthropist, who helps and guides seekers from every spiritual tradition to experience freedom from struggles with anxiety, insecurity, stress, fear, and addiction. Besides giving leaderships to the Way of Love, Juma's World (a charity working with orphaned children in Tanzania), and several companies, David is the author of six books. His latest book, **Awakening To I Am Love:** *How Finding Your True Self Transforms Your Wellbeing, Relationships, and What You Do* *is an unconventional spiritual odyssey about finding love, happiness, and peace from within. To learn more, visit:* https://davidyoungren.com

RICCO MCADORY

BECOMING A FRIEND OF GOD: MY STORY

BY RICCO MCADORY

I f it was up to man's expectations, I would not be birthed on earth. After the birth of my older brother, my mother had her tubes tied and burned to ensure that no more children would be born through her. However, God had other plans. In the fall of 1977, my mother was rushed to the hospital due to an unusual swelling of her stomach. Of course, technology was not as efficient back then as it is today. However, the doctors were compelled to run multiple tests to determine what was happening within my mother's body. After much testing, the doctors were convinced to run diagnostics for a potential baby. Well, the doctors finally saw the reason for the swelling. My mom was carrying me in her womb. What was also interesting is that she didn't know she was pregnant with me until the last three months before my birth. I was born a healthy and strong baby on February 26, 1978, to Robert and Dorothy McAdory in Birmingham, Alabama, at Baptist Princeton Medical Center.

This life story still amazes me to this day. How was it even possible for me to be conceived in the midst of great impossibility? How could the doctors misdiagnose a child for a tumor? Each day that I continue to reflect on this situation, it influences me to praise and worship God even more. Why? Because He thought of me even before anyone else ever did, to accomplish a great work impacting the lives of people.

I experienced my first recognizable encounter with failure when I failed first grade at Grantswood Elementary School. I was diagnosed with a learning disability because I wasn't learning as fast the other students. My parents thought that it was best for me to repeat the first grade. I was embarrassed. Students made fun of me because I was not in the larger classroom with them learning at the same time. Over the years, I grew to tolerate this diagnosis. To help suppress the disappointment, I relied on my athletic ability. Playing basketball was something I really enjoyed.

One day, while in third grade, we were told to sit in rows before we would dismiss from the gym class. I felt very weird and began to pass out. I apparently experienced a seizure. All I remember is waking up in the children's hospital. God healed me and I have not had another seizure.

As I recount these occurrences, it serves as a reminder of how faithful God is. Realizing what He brought me through being conceived in my mother's womb with her tubes tied and burned, misdiagnosed as a tumor, failing first grade, and experiencing a seizure. My life has definitely been an amazing journey so far.

At the age of nine, I gave my life to Jesus. Being the son of a pastor, my dad did a great job leading me to Jesus. At that time, I thought I really knew Jesus, but there were times in my high school and college days when I didn't measure up to being a Christian. Although in high school I did not do drugs or drink alcohol, there were other things that were not the best example of my relationship with Jesus.

In May of 2000, I joined the United States Navy. Before making that decision, my life was not very structured. I even thought I knew everything and did not want to listen to my mom. Life became one frustration after another. My uncle saw the condition I was in and encouraged me to join the military.

He said, "Go into the military and learn discipline so you can grow into a man."

Being in the military was not unfamiliar to the men in my family.

This uncle served in the U.S. Army, as did his brother who retired as a Master Chief Warrant Officer. My oldest brother and cousin both served in the United States military as well. I had planned to enlist in the United States Army like my uncles, however, when I went to the U.S. Army recruiter's door it was locked. Next door was the United States Naval recruiting office. It just so happened they were available, so I went through with the process of joining. I guess their door being open was my sign for me to serve in that branch of service.

I didn't realize that this path would be a set up to the next phase of life that would change me forever. While in boot camp, I learned so many things that challenged my thinking. Even my appetite changed. Whenever we would eat Thanksgiving dinner at my grand-mother's house, I could eat four to five plates of food. During my boot camp experience, I got in great shape, and my meal intake was reduced from four to five plates to two to three.

I could see how much I was growing physically and mentally through boot camp, but spiritually I became distant from the church. When I reported for duty at my station on the USS Carl Vinson (CVN-70) stationed in Seattle, Washington, I started all over. For the first time, I felt free of not having to go to church. For a while, I liked not having to wake up and go to church. I thought I was running away from God, but I ended up having heart issues. They were not physical heart issues, this was spiritual emptiness. I tried my hardest to ignore it, but the more I tried, the more I lost.

In 2001, God used my long-distance girlfriend to win me back to Him. I had met Denise about two years prior to leaving for boot camp.

One day she told me, "I see you as a great man of God."

I enjoyed all of our conversations, but that one comment was not what I wanted to hear. However, she was so beautiful both inside and outside that I could not resist. God definitely has a sense of humor.

I came home in the summer of 2001 for a vacation before we had to leave for a six-month tour of duty. I was met with a great welcome home party from my parents and Denise was there. It was definitely great to see everyone and they all saw how much I had grown up. It was during this time when I proposed to Denise and asked her to be my wife. She said, "Yes!" I was so happy. When I returned from the six-month tour of duty called, "West Pac" Denise and I got married on April 6, 2002.

Where my relationship with God really changed was in 2003. After our ship returned home for a few months, we had to leave on another tour. This one was considered a mysterious tour because we did not know when we would return home. It was said that we could be gone for a year. I was definitely saddened to leave my beautiful queen for so many months. In fact, my heart was more saddened, after receiving the happy news from Denise that she was pregnant with our first child. It was then when I prayed sincerely to God to get me home in time to see Denise deliver our child.

While on this tour of duty in April of 2003, I received my call into ministry to preach the gospel of Jesus Christ. I ran from this call for so long because I wanted no part of ministry after seeing what my dad endured dealing with church people. However, God used Denise to warm my heart, the unknown date of when our ship would return, and the isolation from family to convince me that saying yes to God seemed like the only option.

My faith grew and I learned to trust God beyond what seemed naturally impossible. You may wonder what was so impossible. Well, after studying God's Word consistently during this tour of duty, I declared verbally that I would be home in time to see my wife deliver our first-born son. That sounded good, but the problem was the unknown date of our return was not determined. People made fun of me, calling me a fool for believing God to do the impossible. Regardless of what people said, I still stood on the promise in Psalm 37:4, "Delight yourself also in the LORD, and He shall give you the desires of your heart."

After being told consistently that I was crazy, some possible dates for our return started to be mentioned by our ship's captain. By this time, the discouragement and doubts started to get to me. I was on the verge of giving up, but some of the people who didn't believe me started to believe with me.

They were encouraging me to not give and even telling me, "It's still possible."

So, that night we had a praise service onboard the ship. The praise and worship in that room were so powerful! I began to feel much better and empowered once again to believe. I went to bed with great hope and expectation.

On the morning of September 6, 2003, God woke me up to hear the ship's captain tell us that we were heading back home and should be stateside by September 15. I was elated to know that God heard my prayer. It was, at that time, my greatest faith victory.

The people who had called me a fool now turned around and asked me, "How did you know?"

My response was indeed a platform to testify of God's goodness, "I don't know how, but I know God."

I was approved for vacation and flew home to Bremerton, Washington from San Diego, California. It was such an awesome experience to see my beautiful queen carrying our son. On September 29, 2003, our oldest son, Ricco Sherrod McAdory, Jr. was born.

Whenever I am challenged today with impossible situations, God reminds me of the victory of faith in Him that brought me home in time to see my wife carry and deliver our son in spite of the great doubts of the people around me.

Recently, God revealed and confirmed me as a writer. Now, I knew about the gift to write music, but it was definitely foreign to me about His plan to touch the lives of people with my writing. When I was frustrated with repeated rejection, God reminded me once again of my miracle birth experience and how He brought me home in time to see my son born. It has taken a while, but I am now clear on my God-given identity and the cause He made me to champion. I live to empower others to discover and manifest their own true God-Given Identity by writing about my journey. I pray that my story was helpful to you.

It's great to not only be a son of God, but also a friend of God. He is definitely the best thing that has ever happened to me. My life has more meaning each day because He lives in me. I realize that because

He lives, I can face tomorrow. I know that life is worth living just because He lives.

About Ricco McAdory

In April of 2003, Ricco received his call to preach the gospel of Jesus Christ while serving in the United States Navy onboard USS Carl Vinson (CVN-70). His ship carried the first planes to commit an air strike on Afghanistan.

Ricco is the visionary Founder and President of Davidic Covenant Speaks, LLC and Founder of "The God-Given Identity Experience" Conference. He currently serves as the Minister of Music at Pleasant Hill Baptist Church and as a guest musician and worship consultant in the administration of Authentic Prophetic Worship. He is a Prophetic Minstrel and Songwriter who has ministered before Pastor John P. Kee at the V.I.P. Seminar, Dr. Bill Winston at Tuskegee Christian Center, and Dr. Dorinda Clark-Cole's 2013 Singers and Musicians Conference New Artists Showcase.

He is the author of "The Authentic Worship Leader" and "Discover, Maximize, and Manifest the Real You" Online courses as well as an inspirational speaker and mentor to youth in the areas of identity, purpose, and worship. At the core Ricco's heart is helping the next generation of young leaders embrace their gifts and greatness and release their potential to positively influence humanity.

Ricco McAdory has been married to Denise McAdory for over seventeen years. They are blessed with three beautiful children: Ricco Jr., David, and Trinity. He is the youngest son of Pastor Robert and Lady Dorothy McAdory.

Email Address: riccomcadory1@davidiccovenant.net

To learn more visit: Facebook.com/YourGodGivenIdentity, and www.davidiccovenant.net

PASTOR BOB ENGELHARDT

MY FIRST ENCOUNTER WITH LIVING GRACE

BY PASTOR BOB ENGELHARDT

And these signs will follow those who believe:
In My name they will cast out demons; they will speak with new tongues.
(Mark 16:17)

I was born in the Bronx, New York City, in 1956, the third of seven children, and raised by hardworking parents in the Hudson Valley region of upstate New York. Graduating from high school in 1974, I went straight to work in my dad's business, a small commercial printing company. As a typical child of the seventies, one of my main recreational activity was partying—partying to celebrate weddings, rock concerts, sporting events, holidays, weekends, birthdays, or for no reason at all. My friends and I were not big into illegal drugs, although we had no reservations about drinking alcohol, and did so with a passion. The years between high school and marriage, though admittedly fun, passed in a blur of shallow self-gratification.

I married my sweetheart, Nancy, in May of 1977. She is the best thing (besides Jesus) that ever happened to me. Marrying her was the only smart decision I stumbled into during those years. Besides being in love, we were great partying buddies—that is, until she attended a Jack Van Impe evangelistic crusade just over a month after we were married and gave her life to Jesus Christ. Soon after, she received the "Baptism in the Holy Spirit" including speaking in tongues. She became more deeply committed to God while I continued to view my partying as a harmless form of recreation—something I had no intention of giving up.

It's not that I didn't like God in those days. Having been raised in a church, I always believed in Jesus and had even said a sinner's prayer at one point, ostensibly ensuring my salvation. I even remember nearly having a fight at a party once with a guy who was raised in our church and had become an atheist at college. His arrogance and shallow bitter arguments against the existence of God with his hatred for all churches disturbed me deeply. I let him know, in decidedly unsaved terms, how I felt. So, although I had reverence for God in those days, Nancy's newfound version of Christianity filled with prayer meetings, Bible studies, and praying in tongues was definitely not on my bucket list.

Within the first couple of years of marriage, I began to feel more and more pressure as our babies began to come along and expenses piled up. Now groping to make up time from the wasted party years, in addition to my full-time work, I signed up for college part-time and also took on various menial part-time jobs for extra cash. I then left my father's company and landed a better paying job at another printing house where I worked my way up to manager over several years.

During these years, a very unhealthy shift took place in my recreational partying. Whereas I once felt in control of my drinking, over time, I had a stronger desire to drink myself under the table more often. A couple of drinks became rarely enough. I also began to look forward to these events, planning ahead to my next outing. In the sport of wrestling, there is a move called a reverse. It is when a wrestler is in control and his opponent quickly maneuvers to take the dominant position from him. That was how it felt to me. Whereas I was once in control of the use of alcohol, slowly it seemed to take on a life of its own and I was being drawn into it. I'm not saying I wasn't responsible for my actions in those days—I surely was. Evil, however, once it gets its claws into you, does not like to let go.

In my stubborn weakness, I continued to mess up more and more, frequently making many classic blunders; from wrecking a car to drinking away entire paychecks, to being ticketed for DUI. The greatest damage I rendered, however, was the cost to my marriage. Money was always short and Nancy's family was secretly urging her to dump me. We fought incessantly. Each time after a drunken episode, I was enveloped in a blanket of self-hatred. Despising myself, I would make new promises, vows, and commitments, pledging never to drink again. Always though, after a few days, weeks or even up to two months, my resolve would dissipate and my deep evil self would begin to justify my next outing.

By 1982, our relationship was severely frayed even as Nancy's spiritual life continued to grow. Then suddenly, in the spring of that year, she began to be tutored by a woman friend in spiritual warfare. (This portion of the story is more her testimony than mine.) As Nancy tells it, under this tutelage, she began an ambitious prayer regimen, both in tongues and English, for hours during the children's nap time each day, specifically for me to be radically saved, filled with the Holy Spirit, given the gift of tongues, and set free from alcohol abuse.

Very quickly, faith began to grow in her heart for victory. As it did, I began noticing a change in her attitude towards me. She became very loving and gentle, verbalizing her love, commitment, and confidence toward me and our future like never before. This really confused me because I could no longer justify my actions by reasoning that I needed this alcoholic escape because of my rotten marriage and home life. By Thanksgiving of 1982, I was looking at her Christianity with more openness than I ever had before.

As was our custom, we traveled to Nancy's parents that year for the long holiday weekend. On Saturday evening, Nancy, her mom, and her dad went out to a prayer meeting and I stayed back at the in-laws' house to watch our kids. When they returned home, they had an incredible story to tell. A woman at the prayer meeting, they said, had a personal encounter with Jesus Christ. The woman claimed that Jesus had visited her and spoken to her about a distressful situation she was going through. Lying in bed right next to her, her husband apparently slept through the whole ordeal.

Particularly unsettling to me about this story was not that Nancy or her mother believed it, but my father-in-law, Lou Capra, believed it. Having been a NYC police officer, Pop Capra was as street smart as anyone I have ever known. He could spot a scam a mile away and besides that, he was very suspicious of TV preachers and any religious loonies. So, when I saw how shaken up he was, how this woman's encounter with Jesus had clearly rattled him, it really got to me. I distinctly remember having the thought: *Is this possible? Would Jesus Christ really personally visit a person? Could He do that?*

After years of hearing about God from the church, my wife, my mother-in-law, and her band of wacky charismatic friends, and after months of my wife's constant prayer for me, an awakening of clarity finally penetrated my thick skull:

If Jesus Christ cares enough about that woman to personally come to her, I wonder if He would come to me if I asked Him?

That nagging idea lit a precious flame of hope.

The next evening, we drove the hour and a half back to our home in Glens Falls arriving about 9:00 p.m. After Nancy and the kids were settled in, I left the house telling her that I had to check out the next day's work schedule at the plant. I was really going there for another reason altogether. I knew no one would be working and the print shop would be empty late on a Sunday night. I had decided to go and secretly pray to see if Jesus would come to me like he did that woman.

As soon as I got there, I went to the press room which was down in the basement of the building. After neurotically double-checking that I was there alone and finding an old wooden pallet, I placed it on the floor as a kneeler. (Kneeling was from my church background.) I paced back and forth for a few minutes, trying to stir up enough courage to start.

Finally, I knelt, reached deep in my heart, and very tentatively said, "God...Jesus...Will you please fill me with the Holy Spirit and give me the gift of tongues." (I prayed this way because for almost six years Nancy had told me that this was what I needed.)

As the words were coming out of my mouth, I began to feel a strange tingling sensation on top of my head. Immediately, I was so stricken with fear that I sprang off the pallet and frantically ran to the other side of the press room. Never having experienced anything even remotely supernatural before, I was terrified at the presence I felt. Something was over there! Something I couldn't see!

After a few minutes, I primed my courage up a second time and decided to try again; only this time I resolved to stay with this prayer until something happened. I went back to the same pallet and knelt in the same way and tried to recite exactly the same words. (I had already started a new religion!) I said, "God...Jesus...will you please fill me with the Holy Spirit and give me the gift of tongues." This time when the tingling sensation started, on the top of my head, I didn't move as it increased in intensity and swept over my body.

Some have described this feeling like that of hot honey or warm oil poured over you; all I know is that I was filled from head to toe with the most wonderful, warm, pure, and ecstatic feeling I had ever experienced. At the same time, I felt a pressure pushing up from the inside of me and knew it must be the gift of tongues. I opened my mouth and began to speak as a beautiful new language literally gushed from inside of me. My speech faculties took on a life of their own as my voice continued to surge like a fire hydrant with exotic sounds and I experienced wave after wave of this pure ecstasy. In fact, the tongues continuously poured with such intensity that for several minutes I honestly could not stop speaking this incredible articulate language containing distinct words and phrases, all coming out of my mouth but which I could not understand.

I was so happy that I jumped and skipped like a little kid, running to the men's room to look in the mirror and watch my own mouth talking with this foreign new God-language. I laughed and felt my chin and lips as these cool sounds which did not originate in my mind poured out. All of this was accompanied by an amazing sense of joy. It seemed like every negative thing in me was simply gone. All the self-hatred, guilt, shame, and years of accumulated burdens instantly vanished like an overturned death sentence. I felt like an untethered helium balloon.

But the greatest thing of all was the knowledge that, just like the woman my father-in-law told me about, Jesus came to me when I asked Him. I felt so loved and special and absolutely knew for certain that He was real, that He was a living God/person and that He knew me. I felt reborn! Completely gripped with a profound sense of what I later learned that the Apostle Paul said, "If God is for me, who can be against me?"

I quickly drove home and found Nancy asleep... I had been down at the plant praying in tongues for over an hour!

Waking her I said, "Nancy, wake up! I got it! I got baptized in the Holy Spirit and the gift of tongues!"

She gave me a sleepy-eyed smile and said, "That's good, Duffy."

Then she fell right back to sleep. I was surprised at her lack of enthusiasm because I was thinking she'd get up and throw me some kind of party, but she was so sure by that time of what God was going to do, she took it in stride. I have since discovered that when a mature prayer warrior accomplishes something through prayer when the manifested answer arrives, it's expected instead of a surprise.

That day began the most wonderful adventure in my life. To say I turned on a dime is an understatement. I began running for Jesus with all my heart, and although my take-off was surely shaky, God supernaturally delivered me from alcohol, restored my marriage, and has given me a life of incredible abundance.

I associate my story with a trip I once took to Seattle, Washington, and how overwhelmed I was at the beauty of Mt. Rainier. Rising over fourteen thousand feet into the sky, this snow-capped peak is a magnificent spectacle of God's handiwork. The day I arrived, the sky was blue and the majestic Mt. Rainier dominated the scenery; I could not take my eyes off it. Its beauty seemed to connect deeply with my soul. As night fell on that first day of our trip, I was looking forward to savoring the same spectacular view for the next few days. I was disappointed in the morning to find that Washington's famous rains had moved in during the night and low clouds and fog obstructed the view. So completely was Mt. Rainier cloaked that you'd never guess in a million years behind the flat gray sky stood a dominating masterpiece of God's creation. I never got to see the mountain again on that trip, but I know what I saw!

That is exactly how I know God is real. People can argue faith, philosophy, doctrine, or religion. They can believe or not believe. They can theorize, theologize, and proselytize, but the vast majority are doing so from the fog. They believe but have never seen. I know different. I've seen Mt. Rainier for myself. I know it's there. It's the same way I've experienced God. I called Him, He answered in a way that was more tangible than my eyewitness of that great mountain, and also slipped me His number: my own personal secret code language.

You see, I know Jesus Christ; I've met Him. I'm family. I am a friend of God. We dialogue and communicate with one another all the time. I have His direct line! In addition, having been touched by Him, I have been left with a residue of His presence on the inside of me. So now, when I read the Bible, I sense the same essence as the one who touched me that day. Men can argue over the Bible, whether they believe it or not, but I know it's true. I've met the author and we keep in touch.

Senior Pastor Rev. Robert Engelhardt is a respected author, speaker, radio personality and founder of FaithConnect Leadership Forum. He is noted for his authenticity, biblical insight, and ability to make complex truth understandable. Married for 40 years to beloved wife Nancy who serves alongside him in ministry, Engelhardt has five children, nine grandchildren, and a personal mission to be culturally relevant, biblically sound and genuinely connected.

MIKE "MAC" MCKOY

MUGGED BY JESUS

BY MIKE "MAC" MCKOY

I had always been a God guy, stating hundreds of times over the years, "I don't get this Jesus thing? If I have a relationship with the Father, why do I need one with the Son?"

Asked if I was a Christian, I would respond, "Heck NO! Those people are weird. I am an Episcopalian. Christians were kind of freaky and way too joyful."

Yet, when people asked me about John 14:6, it haunted me.

> *Jesus answered, "I am the way and the truth and*
> *the life. No one comes to the Father except*
> *through me."*

I'd continue ranting on Christians saying, "Well, that verse certainly couldn't apply to me. I'm J. Michael McKoy. I'm 'Special.'"

Holding up my crossed fingers, I'd continue, "Me and GOD are tight."

Oh, I was a regular church attender. My wife and I would get the kids all dressed up, stroll into the church like we were something special. We had "our" seats, third row on the right. I never attended Bible Studies, volunteered for anything, or understood salvation.

Even on My Radio Show, I'd have a Faith and Values program every Friday. We called it, "The View from A Pew." Pastors would come in every Friday and discuss spiritual issues, but I had one rule: "No Bible Verses." I felt that Christians would "proof text" and use the verses and my ignorance of the Bible like a plastic blow-up bat and beat me over the head with it.

They would proclaim: "See there's proof of what I say, that one verse right there. That's why you're bad Mac. You're not a good enough Christian."

There were a few pastors that would really make me think. Pastor Mike Housholder from Lutheran Church of HOPE and Davey Bloom from 2 Rivers Church. God really used them to minister to me, yet, I still wasn't convinced. Why did I need Jesus?

But then on July 20, 2010, **Jesus mugged me.**

I was always a teetotaler, never drinking alcohol until I met my wife. As I recall, she drank especially when we were intimate. Our relationship seemed to be grounded in sex and booze. There was no Jesus anywhere. Then on May 10, 2010, I put the bottle down and surrendered my will and my life to the care of God. I had been sober for almost 90 days when Jesus came to get me.

On July 20, 2010, I was awakened in the middle of the night by my dog standing upright on the bed howling at me. I was sweating and cold all at the same time. When I was able to gather all my senses, I recalled a dream or vision I had just had.

> *I was running to the "light," knowing the light was God and I was going "home." At the last minute, Jesus stepped in from the side, wagging his finger back and forth in my face and said: "I don't know you.!" I have never been so scared in my life.*

I was beside myself and very fearful for several days to come. What did this mean?

Could a relationship with Jesus and the Trinity really be something I needed?

I finally sought the council of several pastors including my mentor at the time, Pastor Richard. He didn't clearly know what my vision meant, but given my, "I don't get this Jesus thing" and my reluctance to accept the Bible verse John 14:6, he said I had better begin to pray for a relationship with Jesus.

So, I did. If I wasn't praying out loud, I was silently praying without ceasing, "God, please give me a relationship with Jesus. God, please give me a relationship with Jesus."

Over and over and over I prayed this. I feared God would punish me and make me wait for the rest of my days to have a relationship with Jesus. After all, I had blasphemed Jesus by denying him for fifty years. Why should God answer **my** prayer?

Then, nineteen days later, on Aug 8, on my way to an early morning Bible study, R.C. Sproul, an Evangelical Pastor spoke to me through a sermon on an RC Sproul PodCast.

I heard: "Hey, God Guy! The Father will 'woo' you into a relationship with His Son Jesus Christ. They are one and the same."

"God and Jesus are the same?" I thought and then RC quoted this Bible verse.

"No one can come to me unless the Father who sent
me woos them to me, and I will raise them up at
the last day." (John 6:44)

At that moment in time, something happened to me. I felt a "peace" and "serenity" overcome my body. Pure Joy. "*Makarios*, God's never-ending and unstoppable JOY!" I have discovered that the feeling I was experiencing was the Holy Spirit consume me. Nothing would ever be the same again.

I called it "mugged" because Jesus took from me the things I felt were important in my life: My Idols—Self-Loathing, Ego, Lust, Guilt, and Shame. Jesus took these things and replaced them with: Knowing God loved me as I am, God's will be done, loving my wife like Christ loved the church and redemption. I had a hunger for the Word and my heartfelt repentant.

Later that day, I was walking to my church office to share my Holy

Spirit moment with Mike, when I saw a picture being hung. I stopped in amazement. It was the face I recalled from my vision—the face of Jesus wagging His finger at me stating, "I don't know you!" It was the very first time I had ever seen a picture of God and Jesus in the same face.

I hunted down the artist, Michael Brangoccio. We have become great brothers in Christ. He shared with me that he too was haunted by that face for years. He told me he wanted to paint Jesus as Isaiah detailed his look in the Bible. Yet, every day when he would go to work on the picture, he felt it wasn't quite done yet. He prayed to God that He would give Mike peace about the picture. He said he wanted anyone who viewed it would see the eyes and expression of Jesus, creating a relationship with the viewer.

A Relationship with the Creator, His Only Son, and the Holy Spirit.

The picture portrayed not only Jesus' humanity but His Divinity. It took him over a year to finish the face, always feeling it was not quite complete. Sometime in later July, in his studio, as he approached the painting, Mike was overcome with the feeling the picture had "come alive" and was indeed what he thought Jesus looked like. It was finished.

The Face of God and Jesus in one... was complete. It was the face I saw. This picture is the most beautiful image I have ever laid eyes on and now I share it with you.

After receiving the gift of the Holy Spirit, I was hungry to read and study the Bible. So, I began to study with a local pastor taking several beginner seminary classes. I thought I was "called" to be this "high-fuluting" Radio Preacher Mac. I mean, I'm on the radio for heaven's sakes, I can certainly give a sermon. However, truth be known, I was a lousy sermon giver. I couldn't go more than eight or nine minutes...just like a segment on talk radio. What God showed me was He had a different plan for my ministry. The question was, how is God calling me to serve?

In 2015, I began to plan a one-week "Live broadcast" from Christ's Birthplace, Bethlehem, on Christmas Eve 2016. Our team arrived a week before Christmas. I didn't hear a voice, but I was standing on a chair at the Wailing Wall. It was Christmas Eve and I was praying in Jerusalem for God to reveal the ministry He had prepared for me. I've got my cross up against the wall and I've got my lips on the cross, praying and praying for God's desire for my life. "I want to serve You. Please reveal Your heart's desire for me as to what You command me to do."

Then something happened. God spoke to my heart. Yet, I didn't hear a voice, I just felt the word: Forgive. While I was at that wall, the Lord laid a word on my heart, one word: "Forgive." *Forgive?* I thought. *Who do I need to forgive?* I knew from Jesus' words that I would be forgiven as I forgave. But I had always been confused about my forgiveness for others. I was perplexed, yet I felt a peace beyond all understanding at the same time. I sat there in awe of God, that He would guide me to my ministry and His will for my life, in Jerusalem. WOW!

Then Craig, one of my travel partners and I walked into Herod's Hall which is just left of the Wall. As we walked in, a very small Jewish man was standing by the entrance. He wore the traditional Jewish clothing: *yarmulkes*, rather larger rounded hats, without brims, a wig (*sheitel*) in order to conform with the requirement of Jewish religious law, black and white with the curly hair braids called *Payot*.

As we walked passed him he said, "You are forgiven."

Craig and I both heard it. I knew that if we didn't go back and speak to this man, I would always wonder was that message meant for me or just his general blessing he said to all.

I approached the man and asked, "What did you say to us?"

He looked at me with gentle eyes and a smile and said, "You are forgiven."

Oh, my, was this Jesus talking to me again? Was my ministry to help others learn to grant and accept forgiveness?

I myself didn't do forgiveness very well. I still carried a whole bunch of resentments. I felt that my wife had abandoned me when I got mugged by Jesus. She told me she didn't want to be married to a man that served God. That's a tough one to forgive, but I would forgive her that next year. Would God really call me to have a ministry of something I knew so little about?

Then I remembered: "God qualifies the called, He does not call the qualified." WOW! I prayed and prayed about His will for me and He had shown it to me at one of the holiest places on Earth, with one simple word and a man that probably was Jesus Himself.

I studied the Bible all the way home on the plane, reading all I could about God's forgiveness and the examples of other men like me in the Bible, learning to forgive. I knew this would be my life's ministry, this book, my PodCasts, my sharing, and my teaching. It would all be about forgiveness.

When I got home, I started the ministry called Forgiveness Church. I now have eleven pastors, plus my own church sending men to me whose lives have been destroyed by unforgiveness. When I run into a man that's just hit bottom, I tell him that forgiveness is the issue. He can neither grant nor accept forgiveness due to his pride. I work with him. It's the most humbling thing I've ever done. That's my ministry and I want to share it with you. I pray you too will be "wooed" into a personal relationship with your Savior. You are the son or daughter of a Risen King and He wants **you** to know Him.

About Mike "Mac" McKoy

Michael "Mac" McKoy is a Christian Radio Talk Show Host & has over 40 years in the Broadcast Industry. hE has written hundreds of blogs on forgiveness, spiritual warfare and his relationship with Jesus. After years of suffering a mental illness that made it virtually impossible to grant or accept forgiveness, Mac surrendered that character defect to GOD and now helps others live a guilt and shame free life. His ministry is to "go into dark places" and minister to the lost & broken.

JEFF GOLDEN

I AM A FRIEND OF GOD

BY JEFFREY C. GOLDEN MSW, LMSW

My story for this book involves the way in which I became aware of and interacted with God. I always knew that God existed. I was brought up going to church and I believed in God always. However, I didn't have an understanding of who God really was or what He meant to us, His creation.

When I was sixteen, my best friend Alan and I were trying to get dates for a summer dance that was being hosted on Grand Island where we lived. There were two best friends, like us, and Alan was interested in the one girl and I was interested in the other. So, we were invited by one girl to come to her house. Now, we lived in Grand Island, which is a very large freshwater island that sits in the middle of the Niagara River. Buffalo is on one side and Canada is on the other. Alan lived at the south end of the island and I lived in the middle. The girl whose house we were invited to lived in the north end of the island. So, Alan rode his bike to my house and then from my house, we rode our bikes to the one girl's house.

So, we get there and we're sitting in the front lawn, talking and kind of just getting to know each other. We wanted to invite them to the dance, but the girls were sitting there trying to tell us how they were different from us.

Alan and I kind of looked at each other and we're like, "Well, we know they're girls, how much more different could they be?"

During the course of the conversation, one of the girls looked up in the sky and she asked me, "What does that cloud look like up in the sky?"

Before I even looked at it, I said, "A dove."

We all looked up in the sky and there in the middle of the perfectly blue sky was a cloud in the best rendition of a dove with its wings outstretched, tail, head, and everything.

My friend Alan looked at me and asked, "How did you know that was a dove?"

I said, "Alan, I have no idea. I don't know how I knew that was a dove."

The girls got kind of excited about the fact that this was a sign in the heavens. Alan and I were a little baffled because it was there. So, a few minutes later, and I looked back up in the sky to see the dove and it was flat out gone. It wasn't there. Now, this particular day, it was warm and sunny. It was late June or early July. There were no clouds anywhere near this image of a dove when we saw it. In the distance, like miles and miles away, there were clouds, but there was nothing anywhere near this dove. So, when I looked up expecting to see it still there, it was gone. I insisted that we get up and walk from the front yard around to the backyard because I figured the cloud had just drifted away like they do in the sky, and we went around the back of the house. That cloud was really gone. It was not there. The sky was blue. There was a breeze and you can see where they go. You can see them move from one spot to another. We're only talking a matter of a few minutes and this cloud was gone.

So, we went back to the front and we were sitting there when the girl's mom pops her head out and said my mother had called looking for me because I was late for dinner. Alan's mom had called my house looking for him because he had an appointment. Alan and I looked at each other. Now, in my house, my dad worked shift work, so when he was home, I was expected to be home for dinner. If you were late for dinner, it was a deal because we didn't get to have dinner as a family very often because of my dad's work schedule. Alan suddenly remembered that he had this appointment for the dentist and it was something set up a long time ago.

Now, this was in 1975 before there were cell phones, so everything was done with a landline. We got up immediately because Alan had quite a ride back to his house and I had to go back to my house. It was about four and a half miles to my house and then another four and half miles to where Alan lived.

We got up and got ready to go, but the girl said, "Oh, no, you're not leaving until we pray for you."

And we're like, "No, it's okay. We really need to get going, we're both in trouble. We need to get out of here."

The girl said, "You know, God is not going to allow you to get in trouble because we were talking to you about Him."

So, Alan and I kind of looked at each other and we're like, "Well, you know, at this point, we're already in trouble, so what's another couple minutes?"

The girls prayed for us and Alan and I were okay with that. We both believed in God, we went to church.

Alan and I had been best friends since fifth grade and we did everything together. So, on the way back, we were laughing and joking about things and talking about this dove and how weird it was that I knew that the dove was there before I even looked at it. That kind of freaked all of us out a little bit that I knew that it was there. Many years later, one of the girls who is still a dear friend and a mentor spiritually, she said she often wondered back then whether I had seen a reflection of the dove in her glasses. I hadn't at all. I just knew that it was a dove.

So, anyway, I went to my house and Alan ran down to his house. We agreed that if we weren't grounded until we were twenty-one, we would talk to each other later that night. Later that evening, the phone rang and it was Alan.

He was all excited and said, "Jeff, I've got to tell you something."

I said, "No, I've got to tell you something."

This is what we shared.

When I got home, because ours was an Italian family, I expected to get the frying pan upside the head because I was not supposed to miss dinner when the family was having dinner. I walked in kind of sheepishly after I put my bike away.

My mother was sitting in a chair reading a book.

She just looked over at me and she said, "Next time you're not going to be here for dinner, let me know. Your dinner is on the stove."

Now that was a surprise too because usually dinner was put away and you kind of had to fend for yourself. It was kind of enforcement of the fact that, "Hey, this is a family thing and we don't get to do it very often." My dad had been called into work. I was in shock.

I was all excited to tell Alan this because this was just beyond anything I could comprehend as a sixteen-year-old kid.

Alan said, "Jeff, here's what happened when I got home."

Now, his mom had always been fair, but yet strict. Alan had a brother and two sisters, and she made sure the family did the things that they needed to do. He fully expected to be in trouble because this was a dental appointment. It was something that was set up a great deal of time ahead.

His mother said, "Alan, if you can't make an appointment that I set, just let me know so I can cancel it and reschedule it."

He said he just kind of shook his head and went up to his room because he couldn't believe that there was no punishment and no anger. There were no lectures, just, "Let me know so I can change it."

We were both just dumbstruck by it because this was so out of the ordinary from what we normally would experience in our families.

A few weeks later, I went to a coffeehouse we had on Grand Island and met Kathy, the other girl, a couple of other girls, and a couple of guys who were all part of this Bible coffee thing. It was about 9:30 or 10:00 p.m. on a Friday night that I gave my life to the Lord Jesus Christ. I could not deny the dove in the sky. It altered the entire course of my life that God interacted with me in that supernatural way. God doesn't always do things in a dramatic, supernatural way, but I think that he needed to get my attention in a unique way. He did.

Now in the forty-plus years that I have been saved, I have not always done it right. I have not always said it right. I rely on 1 John 1:9, which says, "If we confess our sins, He is faithful and just to forgive our sins, and to cleanse us from all on righteousness."

I thank God for that scripture because it has allowed me over the years of mistakes and being human, being disobedient, and being stiff-necked the opportunity to reconcile myself with God. However, that very first time, in August of 1975, that very first time, set my feet on a path. And I have to the best of my ability served God along the course of my life.

Do you know that you can have a relationship with Jesus Christ? It's really pretty simple. God is your friend. We created, "I'm a friend of God" the radio and book program to help you see that there is a myriad of ways that God will intervene and work with people in their lives. All you have to do is give God your attention, believe in Jesus Christ, believe His work on the cross, ask for forgiveness for the things that have separated you from God, and choose to serve Him.

I encourage you to reach out and do that with God because you will not be disappointed just like I was not disappointed.

ABOUT JEFF GOLDEN

Jeff Golden has passionately worked to serve people all his life. He is a licensed Master Social Worker, and is ordained by Cedar Lake Christian Church. Jeff currently practices as a social worker with senior citizens. Together with his close friend, Dr. Larry Keefauver, Jeff hosts the radio program I am a friend of God. The radio program is heard on the message for you 91.7 in Cartersville Georgia serving the Atlanta Georgia, Northern Alabama, and Eastern Tennessee areas.

DR. SUSAN J. BILY-LINDNER

RESET YOUR SOUL™

BY DR. SUSAN J. BILY-LINDNER

Although never having attended church or any other religious, structured programs before the age of five and a half years, I was cognitively aware of my relationship with God towards the end of Kindergarten. I was PS 200, and it was the end of school year term. Everybody was asked to stand up each morning after the pledge of allegiance – day after day – until we had provided the teacher with a response if our parents were sending us to private school or if we were going to stay in public school.

With two other students and myself left standing after over a week of my parents' decision-indecision, I informed my teacher, "I'm going to a Catholic school."

I went home that day and told my mom, "Today, they asked me where I'm going to school, and I told them that I'm going to a Catholic school."

I went to a Catholic school where the structure and regimented classroom setting was a good fit for where I was at this point in my life. My parents and my family were very well-intentioned and loving, but there were deficits from a very early onset in my upbringing and childhood development that impacted my need to find control and orderliness outside the home. I thrived because the expectations were clearly communicated within the academic setting. The education brought forth and reinforced internal strengths and intellectual gifts that may have laid dormant if I had not had the opportunity and learning experience at St. Nicholas of Tolentine. It was an excellent experience for me, setting the tone for my long-term success. My father, in his complete and utter confidence in me, instilled a moral compass of diligence, motivation, persistence, persevering, and never ever giving up. My father's style and "always believing in me," complimented my private school education in ways that I would not truly understand until years later. My mother – who left school early to work and support her family – taught us the love of reading by taking us to the library each week where we took out books that "showed us the world." She remains one of three women I admire so for their propensity for self-education and intellect.

When I was in first grade, the nun told us, "You have time 24 hours a day for yourself, why can't everybody find at least one hour, once a week to go to God's house and pray?" That stayed with me.

It was the winter in second grade that I remember my mom saying, "The weather is terrible. Why don't you skip church today?"

I said, "I want to go to church."

I went to 5:00 p.m. mass alone. Now, I've never heard voices in my head, but I will tell you that in that mass, I listened to a message that basically said, "Susan, your life is going to be filled with trials and tribulations, and it is going to be very difficult, but I will always be with you. I want you to know that in your older years, you will know sheer joy." That was the one and only time that ever happened in my whole entire life.

My parents then moved us during the middle of the school year. They moved me from a Catholic school to a public school. It was a challenging transition for many reasons. We didn't acculturate well because there were a lot of different classes of people with different values systems and morals and different religions. I got moved into more of an elite town, and it just felt very inauthentic. My soul did not thrive, and my inner light started to dim – but the Light never went out. In fact, many times, the light inside of my soul became a flicker. It was very tough from high school through college. I really struggled with always feeling disconnected from God, who had made me in the divine image and whom I had known so well as a child.

I tried in my human form to connect with what was expected of me in the environment that I was born into – confusing values, inauthentic principles, focus on transitory moments that others most likely would have defined as "fun." They say that hindsight is 20/20 and I can assure you that if I knew then what I know today, NONE OF THAT would have mattered to me. I would be like, "I know what's important to me, and I know how I feel. I know where I come from, and that is the only thing that counts." This is a very different world that we're in today. Transparency is the new norm, being accountable for one's actions, thoughts, and behaviors have become a civic responsibility. It was a different world back then. It was tough to cope with being a sensitive spiritual soul in a world where the focus was on materialism and what are you doing in the here and now was based on "fun" and "living outside of the bell curve, in the outliers of "the norm."

For me, having joy in my heart, and having a relationship with God has always been what is most important. I may have strayed far away at times, but the truth remains, my God was always within.

I had a lot of complicated relationships, and I made a lot of bad decisions. My judgment was often skewed because I lost sight of what was in my heart. I had slowly forgotten what was really important to me. Then I remembered and said to myself, "You know what? God is not above me or around me. God is within me." I don't know where this perspective came from, but I believe that God is where there is one big light, and each of us has a speck of that light within us. In the middle of my despair, I realized I had a responsibility to care for this flicker of light inside of my soul because when I care for the light, I care for God. When I care for God, I care for myself.

That was how I moved forward in terms of getting myself healthy, furthering my education, and entering a field where my philosophy, knowledge, and treatment come from both the textbooks and finding my way through my personal struggles. I tell people that our body is the vessel that carries a flicker of light. As bad as things have sometimes gotten, I always have been very cognizant that even if the light was dim, the flicker was always there inside my soul. It was my job to at least acknowledge it. Sometimes, I couldn't take care of it, but I always knew it was there.

Recently, I have had a significant change as I realized I had the calling to do this book. The truth of the matter is for twenty-five years, God has been preparing me to write this book, and the title is, "Reset Your Soul.™"

I remember back in 1998, one of my colleagues asked, "You are trained in Gestalt Therapy and licensed with a Master's degree in Social Work. Why are you pursuing a Doctorate in Psychology?"

I said, "Because the truth of the matter is, this is my calling. I can't explain where it is coming from, but I know that this is my job – the work I came here to Earth to do. I intuitively feel that it is my job to write a book and have a radio show to bring forth the message behind what I have learned in life and through the textbooks. I want to write a book and have a radio show – not because I'm looking for notoriety – but because I feel that this is the work I came here to do. To spread knowledge and information of what I have learned over the last 20 years of listening to people's stories, trials, and tribulations, regrets, and successes. To spread knowledge and empower others with information and resources so that they can make their own independent and well-informed decisions. But to do this, I need credentials after my name to be taken seriously.

I knew that having a Ph.D. in Psychology was very important. I became an excellent doctor because I had incredibly good training and have always been eager to learn, look at myself, and make shifts in how I understand and perceive the world as it continues to change and evolve. My values and morals are unwavering, yet my capacity for resiliency and adaptability to adjust to variables and fluidity of life has always been one of my greatest strengths. I live present-centered, using the past not as a variable of blame but, rather, as a teaching moment to optimize the here-and-now. I always knew this book was inside of me. I've struggled with it. Four and a half years ago, I started to speak to God differently. I began to let Him know I knew that this book was not my book. I couldn't let this book go because this was my job. This is my assignment from God.

I feel that I came through the trials and the tribulations so I would be equipped to complete my assignment. It all makes sense when I look at how everything has evolved chronologically throughout my life. If I didn't know trauma and if I didn't know moments of desperation, I wouldn't be able to share with others, not just clinically, but what it means to "reset your soul" from an emphatic perspective.

What really brings me joy is when I can support others on their journey towards self-actualization in a real and meaningful way - where real and meaningful change happens. This excites me because we are sharing an experience of our interconnectedness and understanding the joy of being human.

When I started writing this book, I also changed the way I prayed to God. I started saying, "Dear Lord, I am no longer going to be praying to You in the traditional way. 'Please bless this one, please bless that one, please help me with this, etc.'"

I said, "I'm done with that because I know that Your way is the way. From now on when I pray to You and when I speak to You, I will ask You to continue to give me the courage and the strength to face the many travesties in the world and bring about change You deem right. I pray for Your will to be done in Your timing. I am here to serve You, and I will continue to keep listening so as to hear Your Will Be Done.

By doing this, I am more abundant in my soul because I am no longer asking Him for anything. I know He has given me everything I have ever needed. I am simply having a Homecoming of my own celebration because the good Lord never ever has left me. I am now vested – despite my fears to be seen and to speak the word of Truth as

I know it - to accomplish my assignment from Him. This is the emphasis of my book and my radio show.

I said this to a patient yesterday, and it astounded him, "I am tired of people praying to God and asking for help with this or that and saying it's all in God's hands. God gave us a brain in order to help Him do His work on earth, we need to hold up our part of the bargain."

We are basically asking Him to do things He's already empowered us to do. I have seen too many people who rely just on religion and God to fix their issues without having the courage to look at themselves. My work is helping and supporting those who genuinely seek Him in their journey and desire to elevate their soul's consciousness to connect with their Creator. That's where we become a friend to God.

God has never left me. He was always there. I knew he was there, but I was communicating with Him as a child does a parent. Then there came a point when it truly became a friend-to-friend type of communication and relationship. Our interconnectedness is more profound because I am now enlightened that He is me and I am Him.

If it's your desire to live life joyfully and to be a friend of God, take a moment to pause and ask yourself, "Am I truly content, not just happy, but truly content in my life?" Think about all the domains of your life: your family, your job, your own personal growth, your friendships, and your education. Ask yourself if you are content with where you are.

One man told me he had a party and there were over a hundred people there. It was his birthday party. He said that he was the loneliest man in the room. It's not about having people around you. It's not about this Facebook moment. It's not about when everyone smiled. It's not about a birthday celebration. It's really about how you feel inside with yourself. Are you living your truth?

The reason people have such discontent is they often place so much emphasis on taking care of or being there or looking out for or giving advice to other people that they cannot look within. Those who cannot look within are the people whom I encourage to stop taking care of everyone else and take care of yourself first. In the end, it's only about you and your Lord. Really what happens is that when someone takes care of themselves and their soul, every other relationship in our human life improves and that is the bonus that nobody expects.

To redirect your life toward a friendship relationship with God, you may be familiar with language like renewing your mind, refreshing your spirit, or restoring your life. Let me encourage you right now to hear what your next step is...

It's time to "Reset Your Soul!"

About Dr. Susan J. Bily-Lindner

"Dr. Susan," brings her expertise as a Clinical Psychologist, Life Coach and Wellness Advocate to support clients vested in finding their truths in order to live with meaning, purpose and authenticity. She is the author of Reset Your Soul^Ò*, a guide to understanding the therapy process and accelerating personal growth. Dr. Susan is also a regular guest on several radio shows and podcasts. Dr. Susan holds a PsyD in Clinical Psychology, an MBA in Organizational Behavior and an MSW in Social Work. She has also completed extensive training in Gestalt Training and Quantum Healing Hypnosis Therapy. Find out more about Resetting Your Soul at www.Resetyoursoul.nyc and/or www.keepinglifereal.com. Look out for Dr. Susan's upcoming radio show, "Keeping Life Real," and supportive resources available on her websites.*

AFTERWORD

BECOME GOD'S FRIEND

Becoming God's Friend is like Befriending God. You publicly turn away from your old life lived outside of God's law and love, and turn toward God receiving His Son, Jesus Christ, as your Lord and Savior.

I invite you to pray this prayer:

I surrender my life to follow you, Lord Jesus Christ. I believe that God raised You from the dead after you died for my sins on the Cross. I repent of all my past sins and receive your forgiveness through the shed blood of Jesus Christ. I receive the Gift of the Holy Spirit. Amen.

> *Then Peter said to them, "Repent, and let every one of you be baptized in the name of Jesus Christ for the remission of sins; and you shall receive the gift of the Holy Spirit. For the promise is to you and to your children, and to all who are afar off, as many as the Lord our God will call."*
>
> — Acts 2:38-39

Your friend...*Dr. Larry Keefauver*